HOPE AND BEYOND

A JOURNEY THROUGH MENTAL HEALTH

SINDHUJA SARASRAM · APARNAA THANIGAI
SANYOGITA BHARADWAJ · KANIKA CHOUDHARY
SREE YELAMANCHI · ANURAG KUMAR · AMOL GAWADE
ARATI HARIKUMAR · SHAGUN SALECHA
VANSHIKA AGARWAL PRITHA SAMANTA · SIMRAN SAXENA

EDITED BY
KANIKA CHOUDHARY

Published by

Inkfeathers Publishing 2020

New Delhi 110095

First edition is published in 2020

Edition Copyright © 2020 Inkfeathers Publishing

Cover Design © Inkfeathers Publishing, 2020

Cover Image © Freepik.com

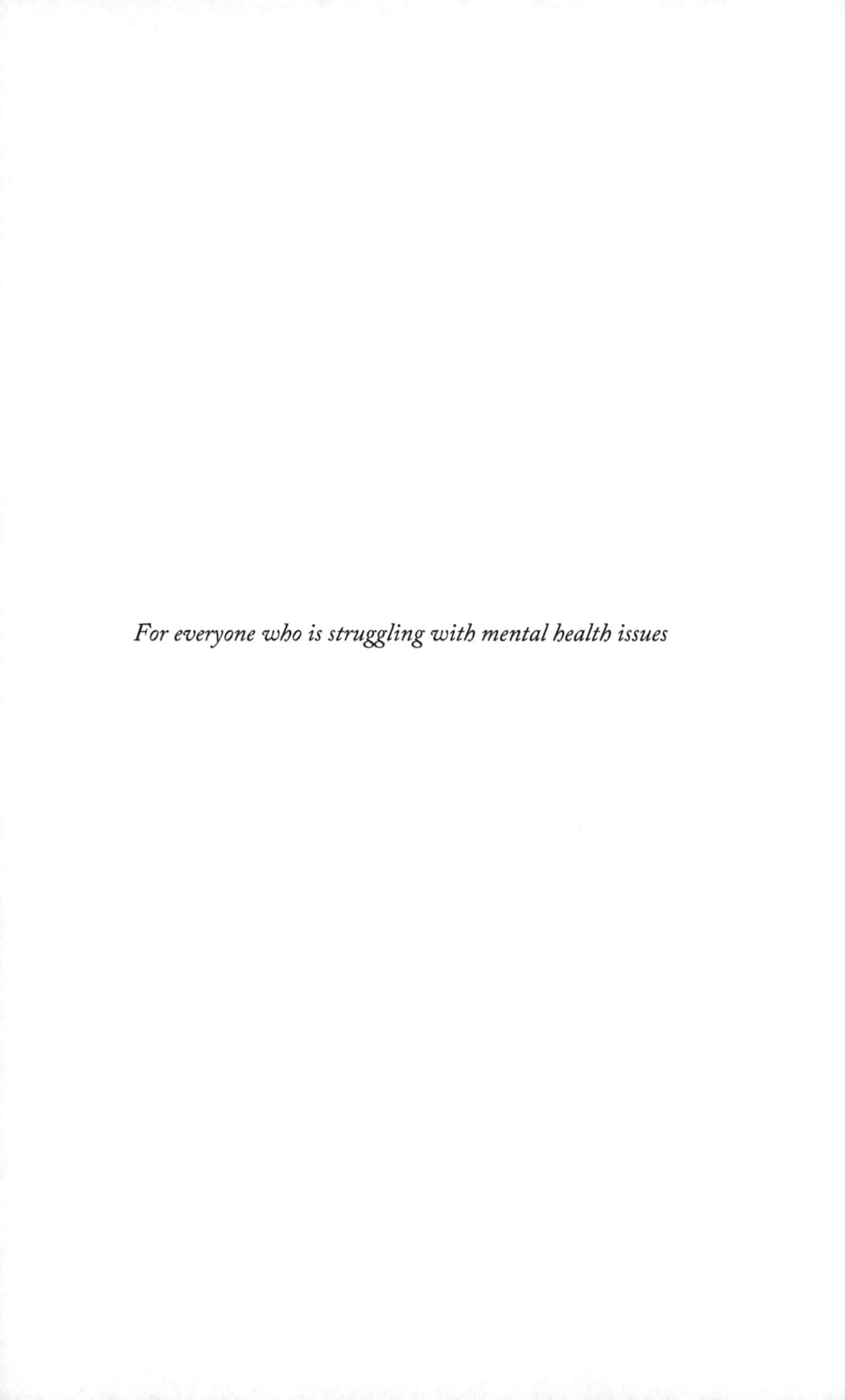

For everyone who is struggling with mental health issues

CONTENTS

EDITOR'S NOTE

Mental health is just an ignored topic in our society, and this is something we generally don't want to talk about but we as a society need to understand the concussion of it. Emotional well-being is equally important as our physical health. It is important to say how we are feeling on our not-so-good days. We need to speak up and share. We need to make it a practice to open up about our bad phases. We need to understand that it is not embarrassing to talk about what's going on in our head and that it is equally important to listen when someone is trying to talk to us. It should not be an option to help someone when it is asked for.

For me, this book ride has been a long-long journey because there aren't many people who want to give their input on their side of the story and display their journey out in the open but I believe when people will read this book, at least 1 person will get inspired and say, "Hey, I went through something like that too" and I guess even if that one person comes up to me and says that then the book is going to be a success for me.

What I want from someone who is reading this book is to feel that you aren't alone in your journey, that there are other people too who are going through a similar phase and it's ok to talk about it, it's ok to break down and feel grumpy but what I also want my readers to feel is the need to speak up, to speak their mind and their experience.

Communication and sharing are something that I believe in and I feel that it is the most important aspect of a healthy life. If you aren't comfortable talking to your parents about it and talk to someone who you know won't judge you. Go to therapies, talk to a professional. Going to a psychologist isn't a bad thing, it doesn't mean that you have gone mental. What I want my readers to do, is to embrace who they are and to not give too much importance to the judgment of the people who don't matter to them in life.

It can get a bit difficult to open up about something that we are so insecure of but that is the challenge, my friend! What good is life if you don't challenge yourself. There are difficult times, there are times when we want to cry out eyeballs out, but I guess it's ok to do that, it's ok to let out our emotions, there is nothing ugly in that. It makes you beautiful when you express that other side of yourself which you have been afraid to touch.

I wish that this book somewhere inspires you, connects with you and gives you the courage to come out to the world. Even if you haven't experienced anything like this before, I hope that you support your friends and family who are going through this, you need to be there for them even if they aren't asking for it. Be someone who people can reach out to and talk about their feelings. Be open and non- judgmental about the situations they are handling; might be important for them.

At last, I just hope that this book makes a difference and the communication just grows stronger and stronger.

Amen.

ABOUT THE EDITOR

KANIKA CHOUDHARY

A vivacious young lady, hailing from Ranchi, Kanika is a travel enthusiast who loves her ukulele and her little notebook of quotes. Taking inspiration from her surroundings, she loves to write and considers writing to be an integral part of her life. Even though the writing was always a part of her school life, she hadn't really taken to it until 2017, when she started her Instagram page called Profound Words, talking about everything she noticed around her. With relatable content, she got popular with readers soon enough and now posts and interacts with her large number of followers regularly. She joined this project with the hopes of learning more about the writing community and getting to interact with different people, each with their own experiences. Having learnt about the process of editing and what goes behind in the making of a book, this experience has been very fruitful for her and she is grateful for such an opportunity, even though she had her share of ups and downs. The book discusses the serious topic of mental health and she hopes that people reading are able to connect with the stories and find comfort in the knowledge that they are never alone, and that even if there's nobody else in life, there's always writing for you.

HOPE
AND
BEYOND

1

A CHANGE OF SEASONS

By Sindhuja Sarasram

◆◇◆

A falling autumn leaf was blown into his eye by the mild breeze. Without stopping, he pulled it off his face and continued his morning run. It was a few seconds before he looked around the park, only then noticing that fall was already here, with the rust-coloured canopies and confetti of dry leaves decorating the drive. This time of the day, he was always zoned in on his routine and the loud workout music blasting in his ears.

After a few minutes, his running tracker sounded as he reached his target of 5.00 miles for the day. He slowed to a jog and kept at it till an empty park bench facing the calm waters of the lake- one that was presented with the sepia-toned horizon. The sun wasn't up yet, and the pleasant weather was tempting him enough to think about staying seated with the vista for the next hour or two.

It was a Tuesday, so he didn't need to be at the gym and only had one client appointment in the afternoon. Even considering some paperwork that had to be done at work, he didn't have to show up before noon. It felt like one of those days when he wanted to stay lost.

As he got home to his tranquil Studio apartment, he tore off his now sticky with sweat clothes from his skin and stepped into the shower. His thoughts were focused on the quiet hissing of the water as it hit his head, ran down the contours of his face, dripping from his jaw down to the rest of him, and the whoosh of the collecting water at the floor drain as it got sucked down. As he walked out wiping a layer of steam from his torso, going over the old scars on his abdomen, he noticed the misaligned foot mat and halted to straighten it out.

He went through his Coffee and Oatmeal breakfast regime as he watched the News on TV, the anchor was droning on about the demerits of the new government and head of state. Tuned out already, he looked towards the kitchen window; a Cat slipped in through the silver of an opening. The vagabond purred and went to her bowl of food with practiced indolence. After she had her fill, she came to wind up on his lap.

It was four in the afternoon and he had freshly showered again for the session. Not considerate of the weather or the client's interests, he usually preferred to be heavily layered like he was at the moment. He had made it clear to Paige that he would take this job only if the topic of his clothing was left to him.

After a few disagreements, she caved in to let him have his because they both knew she desperately needed him to take this up.

He did not feel shy or insecure about his body. One did not feel embarrassed about having a sculpted body like Adonis, after all the hours he pulled at the Gym day-in and day-out. His colleague Jenny openly admired it and so did the other women he sometimes shared a bed with. His discomfort though was altogether for a different reason.

Fresh Linen, scented candles and soft soothing music created the atmosphere to put the client at ease. Right now, she was seated uncomfortably on the edge of the bed, at the side closest to the door where he entered, almost as if she wanted to escape and run from confinement. Yet in her anxiety, she didn't seem to notice his presence. He closed the door with a soft click and that pulled her attention.

"Hi, Anna is it?"

He accepted her incomprehensible nod and said "Hi, Andy here"

"H- Hi" she croaked in her weak voice.

This timid, petite looking girl seemed not a day over 15, much less her actual age of 20. After becoming conscious of sharing the space with him, it only caused her anxiety to spike by the minute. It was pretty clear from first impressions, that she did not make an active decision to come here.

Reading all this, he took a deep breath, he hated new clients, the ones who needed hand-holding, literally and figuratively through the entire ordeal of 60 minutes and if they were anything like this girl, it meant being patient with them for more than one session. The part that frustrated him the most was where he had to take the lead, talk, and get them to relax. He very much wished his regular was here.

"So, is this your first time to Snugglery?" he asked, even as he was irritated by such questions he already knew the answers to. He told himself- it was to break the ice.

"Huh? Oh... Yeah," she said, fidgeting with her palms between jumpy knees.

"Would you like me to play something else?" he questioned, trying to shuffle the music and accidentally started his Classic rock playlist. Disturbed by this out of order situation, he fumbled and dropped his phone that somehow landed between the side table and the wall.

Before he got to change the music or give an apology, she brightened to the instrumental build of a song and surprises him with an assertive "No, that's fine!"

Composed, he figured the music situation to be sorted, sat on the other side of the bed, and asked "So, this is your kind of music?"

"Uh, sort of... "

Noticing that she again drew back into herself with that short answer, he sensed that the music would do the job of de-stressing her before he prodded her some more.

With an abrupt idea, he pulled out his earphones and offered her one earbud as he popped the other into his own ear, "You know, the sound quality is better this way." She tucked the offered earbud, behind her screen of long hair, into her ear. This way, he knew he could sit a little closer to her without barging her space as he inched near her.

Before the singing verses started, he used the time to question her "Um, so do you need water or anything?"

"No, thanks" she replied with a small smile.

Happy with the progress, he assured her "Anna, you can sit back a little more comfortably." Hearing this she moved back maybe an inch, not what he wanted but expected, but he noticed that her posture was a little more relaxed than before.

In his mind, he wanted to let her know that they could go about this slowly, with whatever made her comfortable but the rational part of him liked to remind that they had about 60 minutes to do this session, and 10 of those had already been spent on a non-discussion about Music preferences.

He knew he was being a little impatient, but it was not his job to be a therapist. He only had to establish a level of comfort with her till she could do what he was getting paid for- to embrace, for him to hug her or for her to wrap her hands around him, but in this case, the latter seemed very unlikely.

Mostly, though he couldn't admit this to himself, the events of the past hour before the session started, bothered him. A lot.

As soon as he had stepped into work, he'd sensed trouble by the look of relief on Paige's face. Not much later did he understand his foreboding when she had dumped this walk-in on him, informing that his regular did a last-minute rescheduling of her appointment to Friday.

They were walking out of the office after she quickly briefing him about this client and an unsure voice called out "Andy?"

He'd turned around and was surprised to see a face he'd known very well- "Erin?" the only girlfriend he'd ever had, the one person from his could-have-been life, from before it took a drastic turn.

"Oh wow, it is you!" she said as she walked forward to awkwardly embrace him as he froze.

"Hi, it's good to see you, how have you been?" asked Erin.

"I'm good, how are you?"

"Oh, you guys know each other?" Paige questioned.

While he said, "Yes-", Erin continued- "from high school."

"Erin here, is your new Client Anna's friend and I should remind you that she's waiting for the session. Ah, small world isn't it?"

"Um yeah, Manager actually. Anyways, Andy, I'm leaving this to you, I'll find you later, yes?"

"Yeah...Sure"

*   *   *

The singing verses began,

"...There was so much life in me

Still, I longed to search for more

But those days are gone now..."

And then Anna suddenly choked on tears she was holding.

With this, Andy moved closer to her sideways, now his hips aligned to hers as he held her by placing one hand in hers and the other behind her back to grip her far shoulder. This only increased the pressure on her tear glands as she started weeping breathlessly.

Anna was 18 when she first came to the city, with stars in her eyes. She made the move from her poultry farm small town to the big city. Finding modelling jobs and shared accommodation with 3 other girls seemed easy, finding love... not so much. Within the first 6 months in this concrete jungle, New Year's Eve turned into a date rape for her.

Now, the offender was serving his 14 years life sentence in a prison somewhere, but the mental scars of the event were still etched in her brain. A severe discomfort around men followed this. The romance of the big city life ended for her as fast as it had begun. With no parents or home to go back to, she decided to stay put with the few friends she had collected.

Living off the hefty payout from the conviction satisfied her to stay indoors and not have her personal space interrupted. Worried friends patiently and slowly succeeded in bringing her back to work with therapy, but she only took solo shoots and worked with female designers and personnel whose touch did not push her into a panic mode.

Back in the room with Andy, thinking about her struggle with everything, had her wallowing in self-pity and that brought on fresh heavy tears. It didn't help that he was very subtly and carefully doing his job. All this made her feel like a basket case and she started bawling. After she exhausted herself thoroughly letting out her agony, she realized that now his hand was on her back, going up and down, up and down in a soothing pattern. She was surprised that her subconscious hadn't reacted to this, deeming it as an attack on her space.

It was a good two hours between when she walked in with her friend and Paige got around to understand the urgency, explaining the process, and getting Anna to sign a waiver listing all the rules of engagement.

Only recently did Anna start giving hopes to finding a life partner. Only after therapy determined that she could at least try a little socializing, did she go on the party scene-but very sober and very conscious of the people around her. She never relaxed, much less enjoyed these outings except to satisfy her friends. The anxiety came back when she started dating again, a little innocent cheek kiss, or a brush of hands or a palm at her back led to immediate and awkward endings. There were no second dates.

So here she was, because she needed help, to have it easy around a man's presence.

Now aware, that she was conscious of her surroundings, Andy was glad to know she was taking the proximity well. She removed the earbud and passed it back to him with a small smile, looking into his eyes. He switched the music back to the speakers. Staying where he was and turning towards her, he dropped his hand from behind her shoulders to lay flat his palm against hers and checked with her if it was alright. She nodded her approval and he interlaced his fingers with hers all the time reading her to see if there was any disengagement.

He then suggested, "You can lay your head on my shoulder." as he shifted closer to her with their hips touching.

After a brief hesitation, she tilted her head to rest against his shoulder. He registered what the impact of having one's consent undermined, could do to them. It began with trust issues, where they'd start questioning everybody's motives and the great magnitude of unease they'd feel about asking for help.

He understood this well, for he knew to offer support but didn't know how to take help or seek it. He had succeeded in the art of throwing off any suspicions people around him might have about the hollowness of his life. He wore a mask of the millennial, living the life he wanted and feeling content with it. Only he knew the truth of the matter, an empty house to go back to and a life with nothing he looked forward to.

Almost 18, being a high school senior with- a football scholarship, an early acceptance under his belt, and supportive parents, he knew he had the life most kids his age desired. That summer's vacation turned into a tragedy, deflecting life as he knew it from picture-perfect to a challenge when he lost his parents, his best friend, and his sporting career in one go. He did not get to grieve their deaths as he was mostly unconscious and recovering from his own fatal injuries. A fractured limb and several surgeries led to a long period of physical recuperation. That did not leave much room for attention to his mental health. The insurance money from his parents and the presence of his guardian godfather through the formalities meant he was not thrown into the system. And fortunately, or unfortunately for him, he soon turned 18 and the University even offered a deferral for a year. In the meanwhile, he had all the time to focus on physiotherapy. His busy godfather left him to it with a pat on his back- a promise to visit him often that was not followed through.

*   *   *

Anna's head had switched from his shoulder to the crook between his shoulder and chest. Now his hands circled around her in a warm embrace as she continued to silently shed tears. He placed his head on top of her soft hair and with this, his large frame completely engulfed her body. Maybe that was the reason she did not feel threatened with this closeness- the feeling of a cozy cocoon, so she only let the sadness to spill out into the room.

His attention was on the song in the background. Focusing on music and sound helped him and had always helped him fill up the voids in his thoughts, a replacement for all the stressful things he did not have the answers to. And at times, he needed them as white noise, an ambient for the thoughts processing in his head. So, while his muscle memory went through the motions, his mind was elsewhere. Sometimes, the only source of emotions he felt for, were the stories that unfolded with the lyrics. He no longer knew if it were all that he could feel or that he allowed himself.

Even as he pitied her, subconsciously he understood the craving for touch and help he was too scared to ask for but would accept if offered. Only, his problem was that nobody did, and he was okay with pretending he was alright. Seeing him in her, even if he did not realize it, these were the kind of days that created that need in him. And the thoughts leading to a natural arousal were what he tried to hide from his clients with his heavily layered clothing. These were also the kind of nights that led to one-night stands.

His reminder sounded at 55 minutes and it was a relief for both of them that the session was almost over.

That night, he woke up from a recurring nightmare. It happened on intense days at work, or when he was reminded of the past. But it had been a while since the last one.

He always dealt with this situation in the most primal ways possible- sweat and sex. At the moment, like a reflex, his hand went to his phone to find casual sex.

Walking out of stranger's apartments in the early hours, the morning after was something he did ordinarily. It was easier and helped avoid awkwardness for both parties, and whatever happened between the sheets was clearly defined as a tryst and nothing more. And if a warm body did not help, he worked out at the gym till mind-numbing exhaustion.

He liked this compartmentalization of his life that left little room for mess. He thought he had smartly put them into boxes where there would be an endless outlet for each, not realizing that he was afraid to let someone into his life.

The next week, when he was going through some paperwork, Paige came over with a smile and said "You know Andy, It's nice to see that you know people outside of your gym equipment and folks here." to which he glanced at her and turned back to the screen in front of him. He did not want to comment on that. She was usually the kind of person who did not nose into people's personal lives, but he knew she was about as old as his mother would have been and sometimes acted on her maternal instincts towards her younger colleagues. Only, he had never encouraged any bonding of that sort to take place and didn't want to start now.

"So, have you called her?"

"Who?"

"Oh, who else could I be talking about? That girl, Erin! Jenny was cribbing about you fraternizing with Clients- which I know isn't true, and you're acquainted, so I assured her this was different. So, have you called the girl? I heard she wanted to treat you to lunch."

"No, I haven't," he said, not that he felt obligated to give her an answer.

"Well, you should! I feel like something's there... did you kids date in high school?"

"Umm... yeah, we did, but that was a long time ago" he didn't even know why he was saying this out loud. Sure, he thought about her for the rest of last week but talking about it to someone else was so out of character for him.

"Who knows, you could always try. At least, for old time's sakes and it's just lunch. When you look the way you do, you have to connect with old friends or flames to show off, just saying. You know, Jeff and I were just friend in high school, but meeting at our 10th-year reunion..." she'd started but the rest of which he'd tuned out, thinking about how Erin still looked the same as she did back then, a gentleness about her face and eyes that were so captivating.

He remembered how, just after they were celebrating their diplomas, he told her they should break up. And as positive as she was to try, he didn't think he could do it, the long-distance relationship they had planned. He remembered the pain he caused, but as she took it courageously, he did not feel guilty about it. He was young and stupid.

"And don't think I didn't notice. It's like you don't know how to embrace outside of a timeframe of 60 minutes and an 80$ bill. You need to find somebody, Andy"
He looked at the card Erin gave and thought it was time for a long-overdue apology.

Not sure how he looked, or if the little bouquet was a bad idea, or if he made the right choice with this restaurant, Andy was under the duress of making a good second impression on the girl he'd known the longest.

In all of 5 minutes, he started feeling the urge to get it over with, then he spotted her approaching from across the street- her silky black hair in waves framing her face, an expensive jacket thrown across her shoulders. In a t-shirt and skinny jeans, she walked in pace with the busy city.

She waved at him as soon as she entered the door. Approaching closer to their table, she got near enough for his side hug- that he was sure to deliver, to relieve himself that it was not a big deal. He then handed over the flowers. "Hi," he said, this time, feeling like he could do it better since he was prepared.

After they order their lunch, "So Andy, tell me. How did you get into Snugglery, I'm curious? Sorry, but it's hard to picture you other than that type…"

"What type would that be?" he could take the teasing.

"Oh, you know… I've only seen you in your adrenaline glory on the field … always the fist-bumping, and chest slamming types"

"Ah, the Andy and Adam show!" he said, and she regretted her line of questioning. So did he, with his answers. She tried switching back with "You haven't answered my question."

"Well, that happened by accident. There was some mismanagement when a stand-in receptionist got confused between the schedules of a colleague, Andie with an 'I' and mine. So, I ended up at the door of someone I thought had requested me for personal fitness training. As soon as the door opened, this woman in her 40s pulls me into an embrace and starts tearing up-"

"What, for real?!" Erin asked with hands over the smile she was trying to suppress.

"Yeah, and she's continuously at it that I can't even address the confusion. Meanwhile, I put it together in my head as to what actually happened, but by then it was over 40 minutes that this woman had me suffocated and drained of all blood in my upper body."

This sent Erin into a fit of laughter and he couldn't help but feel glad for it and embarrassed at the same time. He was puzzled by this lightness he felt while talking to her.

"So how…" she said before she had to check her laughter. He then volunteered the information "So, after that woman gave such positive feedback about me, Paige, whom you've met, almost arm-twisted me into getting a certification for the job. Because I met the standards of 'The Dream-Material' type cougar clients desired."

Hearing this, he could see that she was biting her cheeks to keep from laughing. As soon as he gestured to her that it couldn't do any more damage, she broke down to giggling uncontrollably.

After she got her composure back, cheeks still stained red, he struggled to come up with what he could say. And as he was thinking, she said, "Andy, I'm so sorry about what happened."

"Oh that…that was a long time ago," he said, playing it off.

"I found out much later, as I did not keep in touch with anyone when we moved West… I didn't know."

"That's alright, and you certainly don't owe me anything after the way I ended things between us… I'm sorry."

"No, it took me some time, but I realized where you were coming from. I can't hold it against you. But Andy, we were friends before we became anything else. I would have been there for you and finding out that you lost your parents and Adam at the same time, it just broke my heart that I didn't even know what you were going through."

"Hey, you didn't know… and I'm still here."

"But I found out a year later, but couldn't get in touch with you and it really had me worried."

"I… I didn't know that…. I felt so lost, so I packed a bag and travelled about… Thought I'd find myself," he couldn't believe how words were spilling out of him so easily, all those thoughts he never voiced in all these years.

For the question in her eyes that she hesitated to ask, he said "It did not quite help… so I landed back here when I tired myself out… I somehow got obsessed with fitness after it became a struggle following the accident. So, I wanted to overcome that- it became a priority. After that I got myself certified in athletic training."

"You know, it's really great to see you here overcoming all that and, by yourself. Your parents would have been so proud of you."

"Thanks, I guess," and after a brief hesitation he said, "I'm really glad we could catch up."

"Me too," she said as her eyes seemed to convey the same.

*   *   *

Their lunch ended prematurely when she suddenly got a work-related call. He looked at the time and realized that he didn't even notice how much time had passed while they were catching up over the missed years and he was going to be late for work. They decided they'd keep in touch, as they both hurried towards their impending schedules. Nevertheless, Andy seemed to look less dead that evening, as noticed by Tonya, the receptionist, when he entered the Health club.

Andy's thoughts were preoccupied with the afternoon; he understood how much of a difference it made to have someone familiar, to have someone to talk to or to be understood.

*　　*　　*

He was on the back seat, his best friend next to him, both singing loudly to the beats "We will rock you" along with his dad who was driving. "Oh, come on you boys, take a breather! Are you all really not exhausted singing at the top of your lungs?" his mom asked to which Andy only increased his volume. "You know some of us do like the silence," she said trying to hide her smile and sound irritated. "Oh, you fooled me there, college-days-hippie-Linda!" said his dad with his grinning face to her.

Suddenly, the four of them turned to the bright headlights hitting them through the windshield. "Dad-" Andy saw everything that happened right then- in slow motion and clear detail. Their car came to a screeching halt, the unfocused eyes of the other driver and his car that was edging fast and closer to jam theirs, head-on. The impact of the collision and the crushing of the front end he saw, behind the now blown-up airbags in the front, the parents jerking forward in their seats as the shattering windshield glass fell on them. The car rammed sideways into the curb, crushing Adam, and pushing both vehicles into a spin. He could see his parents' heads lolling.

He began to call out to his parents, but he couldn't hear his own voice. He tried over and again, but he couldn't make a sound.

He woke up with an angry hiss of- "MEOW!!!" Chest heaving from the panic, he came to his senses, felt around him in the dark to realize he was there in the comfort of his bed. Still angry and shaken by his sudden throw, the cat was still growling. Feeling suffocated in his perspired state, he pulled off the blanket to get out.

In the kitchen, gulping down an entire bottle of cool water, he could feel a burning sensation somewhere on his chest. He looked down to see her claws had gotten to him. Looking at her eating her food, wary of him, he said, "Sorry Cat," and she still hissed her discontentment. Realizing his need to get it out of the system, he picked up his phone to find a Tinder hook-up.

Five minutes later, he was down the street to hail a cab. As an empty cab slowed down for him, he gave directions "5th on the West, 46th street, please" and climbed in. He looked at the girl who'd swiped right with him and he wondered what made her opt for this tonight, at what must have been her story.

He then reminded himself not to delve into that. He didn't need to know about her to sleep with her.

After a few minutes, the cab halted and the driver said: "We're here, Man, where to?" Only then, Andy switched his attention from his phone to his surroundings.

"Hey, where are we? I asked you to take me to 33rd East…"

"C'mon man, you said 5th and West… so here we are on 5th and West, you gotta go somewhere else? I'll take you… just as long as you pay up for this"

"Know what, never mind, just drop me off here," Andy said as he opened his wallet to hand over the driver a bill. "Thanks."

With that, he got out onto the sidewalk lit by the streetlamps as well as posh apartment lobbies spilling light onto the pavement. He walked a little further from where his cab dropped him, trying to compose his thoughts and figure out why he gave this address.

Suddenly he felt agitated as he remembered what address that he'd given the cabbie. It stressed him out to work out why he'd done that. It stressed him, even more, to think about what he was going to do now that he was here. He felt sweat beading his forehead as he tensed up, a difficulty with breathing as he plainly had no idea what he was doing here. He definitely wasn't here, expecting Erin to have sex with him, just because they bonded over lunch earlier in the afternoon.

He stepped down on to the road and plopped himself on the sidewalk, dejected that he couldn't figure out his needs at that moment. With his elbows on his knees, he dug his fingers into his buzz-cut hair, as if he was trying to connect physically with his brain and get all the answers he needed right then. At 2 am, the scent of lust and the drunken daze of youth and plenty seemed to blanket over every living thing on the sidewalk. In that surrounding, he wished he had someone next to him, to offer comfort. While he was under this turmoil, a withered leaf swept by the wind, landed slowly in front of him.

At this moment, he understood. He was here because he wanted to break this cycle- the emptiness he felt as he offered someone else guidance, strength, confidence and comfort, the addiction for physical exertion, casual sex, and the following emptiness. He was tired of everything, and he knew it only too well. And here was this opportunity, someone who said they were here for him if he needed them, only did he know how desperate he was to take up on the offer. For a change he'd like to ask for a hug, take what he wanted and not the other way around. On the other hand, he knew how much he'd lose if he ended up back where he started. He knew he'd never survive it again.

Among the many feet walking on this avenue, ignoring a guy bent over himself, one pair of stilettos slowed down as it reached nearby.

"Andy, is that you?" came a voice.

He looked up in surprise to see just the person who caused so much conflict in a matter of days.

"You know, this is the second time I've found you in a week's span, I swear I'm not stalking you," she said with a little sparkle in her eyes.

While she gazed at him, his eyes found on the wrinkled leaf. With a whimsical smile, he now turned to look at her with a calm he seemed to be getting re-aquatinted with.
She noticed something was off, placing herself on the pavement next to him, she asked, with a hand on his nearest shoulder "Are you okay?"

He took a few minutes before he answered, "No, I'm not". And immediately, he felt a weight off his chest.

*IT IS JUST A PAGE AND YOU ARE ONLY HUMAN SO
JUST DO WHATEVER YOU WANT TO DO ON IT,
SCRIBBLE, TEAR IT IN HALF OR MAYBE JUST DRAW
SOME LEAVES.*

2

THE BEGINNING OF KAI

By Aparnaa Thanigai

◆ ◇ ◆

PART 1- EMERGENCE

Let me start by saying, this is not a fairy tale. Although they do have some common elements. Damsel in distress- check, helpful dwarves, and mice- check, happy ending-now this is tricky. It's possible, don't get me wrong, but do we know what happens post happily ever after? So, let's hold off on that one because they might just end up emulating reality. But you know one thing that is starkly different? Knights in shining armour can also be in distress and they need to slay their own demons before rescuing their princesses. But I digress, where was I? Once upon a time, I apologize, I'm asked to begin this way. But really, this story takes places in a not so distant past. I also apologize in advance for the rambling nature of my storytelling.

Picture this- it's a glorious morning, the sun in its majesty shyly peeking out, the cerulean blue sky framing it like a prized painting in Louvre. The slumbering city of San Francisco jolts awake like a machine, slowly but powerfully. The golden gate bridge glints brightly and for a lack of better word - 'orangey' under the sun. Out of its thousands of residents, I would like you to meet someone. His name is Kai and unlike the city he lived in, his day hadn't begun yet. He lived in the neighbourhood of Haight-Ashbury, the aftermath of the counter-culture movement that clung to the bygone times unyieldingly. In one of the brightly coloured Victorian houses, standing proudly like sentries against invisible enemies, he slept like there was no tomorrow like he lived in another world that only he had access to. So, he slept on, even as the clock ticked, sweeping away swarths of time, even as the coffee machine thrummed to life, even as the occupants of the house got ready to face the new day.

As the clock struck 8, Mama Duong sprang up the stairs to wake her eldest son before she left for work. She banged on her son's door because nothing less than a pandemonium can stir him. She loved him, she did, but sometimes she couldn't recognize who he was or where he came from. He's nineteen, he sleeps all day, he barely makes it to his classes and if not for the fact that he was a carbon copy of her husband, she'd think he was switched at birth. It made her guilty to think of it, but sometimes she wished he was more like her younger son Hanh.

"Kai, wake up! you have a class in another hour. I don't want to come back home and see that you haven't moved from your bed!" yelled mama Duong.

She could hear the rustling of sheets, trusting that Kai would be responsible for once, she left in a hurry as she could hear her husband honking from the driveway.

"I'm coming!" she whisper-yelled to herself.

She grabbed her bag, slammed the door, and got into the car. "You didn't have to honk so many times" she scolded her husband.

"I had- I am late for a meeting. I am getting sick of this routine every day. He is nineteen and he should be able to get himself to his classes without his parents haranguing him. Did he wake up?" asked Papa Duong

"I think so," replied Mama Duong vacillatingly.

As they drove away, concern and disappointment for their son lingered in their minds.

Meanwhile, Kai slowly stuck his toes out of his blanket, stretched his hands and opened his eyes. The thought of getting up and going to class making him feel like Atlas, forced to carry the entire world on his shoulders. His body felt heavy like an anchor and his mind, slow and lethargic. He shuffled out of his bed like an old man, ignoring the shadow in the room. He threw on his clothes and got ready for his class. He had already missed a few and if he wanted to pass, he can't afford to miss anymore. He took a fortifying breath, already dreading the day ahead.

It was 5 minutes before the class started and the room was abuzz with tittering students. Ayra slid in beside Kai, sweaty in her eccentric gloriousness. She wore ripped jeans and fishnet stockings, a polka-dotted dress brushed the middle of her thighs, her red combat boots, and a tattered denim jacket finished her look. Her technicolour hair vying for attention with her colourful personality as if that could ever be possible.

"Betrayed by my alarm!" Ayra exclaimed as an explanation for being late.

Kai nodded as if this wasn't their routine whenever he managed to make it to class. In fact, that is how they met. On the first day, when Kai, as a freshman made his claim on the seat at the back of the class, Ayra slid in next to him just before the professor closed the door. It had been two years since that fateful day and since then Ayra has claimed Kai as her own. Kai didn't mind this one bit at all. It saved him from the painful process of making friends. In fact, he was grateful for her friendship, even if sometimes she overwhelmed him.

"Surprised you made it to the class," Ayra said distractedly while she rummaged in her bag for a pen.

"Yeah, well I thought I'll shake up your boring life by turning up" quipped Kai.

"Smartass! Also, can I borrow a ......"

She trailed off as she looked up from her bag to the pen that Kai had already placed in front of her.

"Thank you," she said sheepishly.

"Why do you even bother to look? You know you always forget!" said Kai.

"You'll never know when you'll surprise yourself Kai," Ayra said sagely.

They turned to the front as Mr. Rutherford began the class. Kai started tuning out European history and began doodling on his book. He was startled from his trance when the bell rang, signaling the end of the class. Students were milling towards the door when Mr. Rutherford called out "Remember that the list will be posted tonight!"

Kai turned to Ayra "List?"

"Yeah, for the group project," said Ayra.

Looking at the clueless expression on Kai's face, Ayra groaned. "Seriously Kai, you need to start paying attention in the class! He was talking about our final project and he's assigning everyone a partner. The list will go up tonight"

"Oh" Kai uttered as understanding dawned on him.

"Yeah, oh!"

"Do you have any other class today?" asked Ayra.

"No," he answered.

"So, do you want to grab lunch?" Ayra asked.

"Nah, I think I'm just going to head home."

"Are you sure?"

"Yeah, not feeling it," said Kai while eyeing the shadow from the corner of his eyes.

"Suit yourself. Catch you later dude!."

'What's in your head zombie' by Natalia Josh blasted through his headphones, as Kai walked home.

*　　*　　*

PART 2 – SLUMBER

A chime woke Kai up from his deep sleep. His room was lit up by a computer screen displaying an email. It looked like he was about to find out who his partner was. He was praying it would be Ayra. He plopped down in front of the computer and opened the mail. He scrolled through the list and found his number and …Alana. Alana Harrods. Now I need to give you a low-down on Alana. Alana or Lana is the day to Kai's night. How does she differ from him? Let me count the ways (it's a poetry reference, get it?). For starters, she brimmed with joy and exuded light. She also lived life with exuberance, throwing herself at it like there was no tomorrow. Now any other guy would've been thrilled to be paired with Alana, but Kai? Not so much. If you asked him, he would vehemently deny but he might have a teeny tiny crush on her. Now, this posed several complications to Kai's world, the foremost being her knowing his existence.

He picked up his phone to message Ayra when Mama Duong called him for dinner. The three of them were already at the table when he took his seat. Dinner consisted of chicken Pho and Goi ca, a Vietnamese green salad. As they served themselves, Mama Duong looked at Kai.

"How was your day?" she asked.

"It was fine," replied Kai.

"What do you mean it was fine?" she prodded.

"Just that," answered Kai noncommittally.

"Kai!" Papa Duong admonished.

Kai sighed. "It was good. I have an assignment due at the end of the month." he remedied his answer.

Mama Duong turned to Hanh "What about you dumpling?"

12-year-old Hanh, even on the verge of adolescence revelled in his mother's attention with childlike glee. As Hanh regaled his parents with the splendour that his day was, a peculiar phenomenon happened. Kai retreated into himself like a turtle into its shell. He excused himself and sort refuge in his room. He had a lot to think about and a lot to worry about too. After all, it's not every day that Kai was going to meet Alana Harrods.

The next day Kai got up to the dawn of a new day and not his mother's hollering for a change. He hadn't slept well and though that wasn't an oddity in itself, being a nervous wreck was. If I can speak for him, he had a case of jitterbugs and nervous energy scrabbling for an outlet. He reached his class with the same constitution. He took his usual seat and waited for Ayra.

He had a plan, well it just had one line. It was "Don't mess this up, Kai!"

The class ended before he knew it. He told himself "Now or Never". He bid Ayra goodbye and walked down the stairs. Alana looked up just as Kai reached her. She had long brown hair that complemented her caramel skin. She wore a graphic tee shirt that said "Live Today" over ripped jeans and ankle boots.

"Oh hey, Kai! I was just coming to speak to you," said Alana.

"You know who I am?" Kai sounded surprised.
Alana laughed and said, "Ignoring the fact that we're in the same class, you're also the only Vietnamese guy around here, so yes Kai, I do know you."

"Oh yeah, that makes sense," Kai replied sheepishly.

"Do you want to grab some food while we talk about our project?" she asked.

"Sure. Do you have any place in mind?"

"Hmm. What about that new deli down Nicholson's? They're supposed to have sandwiches to die for."

"That sounds good. I don't know about you but death by food sounds great!" countered Kai.

Laughing, Alana headed out and Kai followed her. He secretly congratulated himself on what he considered to be a successful introduction. And he patted himself on his back for making her laugh.

They got their sandwiches and sat at their table. They munched on their sandwiches in silence.

Alana scrutinized Kai as they ate and observed: "You don't talk much do you?".

"Mmm, not really," replied Kai.

"Well, that is going to change my friend, because I am a talker with a capital T. And I don't like having one-sided conversations responded Alana.

Kai grinned and said, "I'll consider myself warned."

Alana spoke as they ate. About everything and nothing. She would be talking about their project one second and about her neighbour's dog the next. No one ever spoke to Kai the way she did. Not even Ayra. Her conversations felt like rain on a hot day, a cool breeze that soothed your soul.

They paid the cheque and walked out.

"What about this Saturday? I can come to your place and we can start working on it?" asked Alana.

"Sounds good but can we do it at your place instead?".

"What are you hiding that you don't want me to know Kai Duong? I'm kidding, but we can't do it at my place. I stay in the dorm and my roommate isn't big on guests." explained Alana.

"Oh, that's alright then. I'll message you my address." he conceded.

"Is this your way of asking for my number?" teased Alana.

"Ugh no…" sputtered Kai.

"Chill, you're so easy to rile." laughed Alana.

"Give me your phone," she demanded, holding out her hand.

Kai handed his phone to her and watched Alana feed her number into it.

She returned the phone and called out "Later Duong!" as she left.

Kai stood in front of the deli and watched her walk away, unable to believe what had just happened. That day even though sleep claimed him, his dreams were pleasant for a change. The week that followed was probably the best week of Kai's life. Alana came over on Saturday and fortuitously his brother had a soccer game, which meant Mama Duong couldn't meet Alana.

Mama Duong, though well-intentioned, either turned any social visits by Kai's friends, few and far in between they might be, into interrogations or made it awkward by fawning over them, as if Kai having a friend was a cause for celebration. Alana and he started working on their project with full steam, but it was not all just work. Kai felt he had a new purpose to wake up every day, even if somedays felt bleak and dreary. Alana was a glimmer in the horizon that poked holes into the blanket of darkness he surrounded himself with.

It's funny how easy to talk to she was, even if she did most of the talking. It felt like she was on a grand adventure and she had picked him to come along for the ride. Even Ayra, whom he had been friends with for two years, never fit so well. But to be fair, she did try. Ayra had a habit of adopting outcasts and society's misfits. One look at Kai, she recognized a kindred spirit. But Kai never let himself open up to her completely and Ayra didn't pry. But that wasn't the case with Alana. She unabashedly pried into his business and she did it so charmingly that you forgot to be affronted or uncomfortable.

One day in class, he was texting Alana when Ayra caught him smiling at his phone.

"What are you smiling at?" asked Ayra.

"Nothing," replied Kai.

Ayra had a look on her face that Kai had never seen before.

"What is it?" asked Kai.

Ayra just shook her head.

"Come on, tell me" insisted Kai.

"You know in the two years I have known you, I have never seen you smile like that."

"I smile," defended Kai.

"Not the way you just did. When you smile, it seems like an effort. Like you have an anchor pulling you down and you're barely staying afloat."

Kai remained silent.

"It's a good thing, right?" he asked after a while.

"A very good thing!" she replied.

"So, do you like her?" she asked after a while.

"What? No!" Kai denied vehemently, even though the blush on his cheeks gave him away.

"Methinks thou doth protest too much".

"Stop it!".

"If you say so," Ayra replied in a sing-song manner. She looked at him, trying to read his mind.

"Can I ask you something?" she asked.

"Sure."

"Do you really consider me as a friend?" Ayra asked holding her breath.

"Of course, I do! What sort of question is that?" Kai asked looking offended.

"It's just that Kai, you never really want to do much with me. You don't talk to me and I mean really talk to me. It has been two years and you haven't even invited me to your house. And as far as I know, I am your only friend. I don't get you!" Myra exclaimed frustratedly.

Kai looked down guiltily.

"You're not my only friend," he said softly.

"What?"

"You're not my only friend. I just haven't spoken to the others in a while. And believe me, I haven't invited you home for your own good."

"Why?" persisted Ayra.

And he knew she was asking about more than what he had said aloud.

He knew she deserved more, but the silence was what he could give her. He didn't know if it was because he didn't know the answer or because he didn't want to face it. He was afraid to look closely. So, he remained silent.

Ayra sighed and turned away. The class ended and they walked out together. Things had changed, words unsaid were said and I think it broke a truce that had gone on for too long. Ayra waved at him and left without another word. Before he could take another step, someone hurtled into him.

"Guten Tag Kai!" Alana said enthusiastically.

Kai raised his eyebrows quizzically.

Alana humphed and said "You took the fun out of it. It means 'Good Day' in German."

"Oh! Why didn't you just say that in good old American? And weren't you learning Spanish last week?"
"I was. I am taking a break from it and learning German now," she said like it made perfect sense.

Kai shook his head and said, "I don't know how to keep up with you."

"Well for starters, you can keep up with me by taking me to your place".

"We're working on the project today?" he asked as this was news to him.

"Nope, we're going to hang out."

Kai was so startled by this news that he couldn't do anything but follow her. Why, he didn't even have the time to be nervous!

*　　*　　*

PART 3 – AWAKENING

They were in his room and he didn't know what to do with himself. He was standing by the door, watching Lana take in everything. Though she had been to his house before, she hadn't seen his room. She muttered words like "interesting and "who would've thought?", which just served to make him feel like he was on trial. Kai's room was sparse and utilitarian. But what he lacked in furniture and other knick-knacks, he made up for it with art. To be specific, his art. While Kai might have been shy, his art was loud. There were gruesome abstracts in black and white, bold red fighting for dominance with sunny yellow, there were beautiful pink cherry blossoms and chopsticks next to a dragon breathing fire, there were quotes and poems and much more. It was wonderful chaos reflecting what Kai was really like inside. No one had seen his room in the last couple of years. It felt like his chest was being cracked open and his heart bared for her to see.

At last, having had her fill, Lana turned to Kai.

"Kai, you artistic genius! Why aren't you in art school or some European country making it as an artist?" she asked.

Kai exhaled for the first time since he entered the room. "It's difficult to make a living as an artist. Besides, my parents are paying for college and they wanted me to do something practical."

Alana just blinked at him. Unable to comprehend that something as practical and silly as that was stopping him from doing what he loved.

"But you could have an exhibition, do it part-time you know? And if you make enough money, who knows?" she reasoned.

"It's not just that. These paintings are private and showing it to anyone would feel like ripping my heart out and letting people dissect it."

"I understand, but don't you think that's what differentiates a painter from an artist?" countered Lana.

"Maybe," answered Kai. Eager to change the subject he asked, "So, what do you want to do?"

"I can take a hint. But hear me out. What if we start small? Maybe you can illustrate something for our project?".

Kai gave it a thought. It wouldn't be personal, and Mr. Rutherford would be the only other person to see it…

"Okay I will, but only if you promise to drop the subject." he acquiesced.

"Deal! I'll drop it. For now." she said determinedly.

*　　*　　*

The next few weeks were a strange time in Kai's life. It brought certain someone closer to him but at the same time, it took someone away from him too. He was happy though. After a long time. He spent a lot of time with Lana and it wasn't just about the project either. They hung out and watched movies, went out to eat, she even met his mother and it wasn't as disastrous as he had feared. He was doing his art and even if it was just for the project, it made his heart sing. She was unlike anyone he'd known. When he thought he had her pegged, she'd pull the rug from under him. And he can finally admit to himself that he liked her. She brought colour into his monochrome life. What can I say? I am cheesy. She even made him forget the shadows for a moment. He had been getting through life until he met her, one day blending into another, waiting for something to change. And she was that change. Her zest for life, unbridled enthusiasm about even the smallest thing made him want to experience life as she did.

Kai had had a few girlfriends in the past. Way in the past. When he was in high school. None of them lasted more than a few months and he hadn't dated since university. The more time he spent with her, the harder it seemed to not blurt out his feelings to her.

A week after they had submitted their project, Kai didn't attend his class. The shadows were particularly dark that day. He closeted himself in his room and didn't leave his bed. He slowly awakened to his door fighting for its life. It was being manhandled by one Alana Harrods. He opened the door wide and let her in. Her face was a picture of worry and anger.

"Why didn't you come to the class? And why didn't you answer your phone?" she asked, firing one question after another.

"Sorry, I was sleeping. Not feeling good," he replied, looking tired and morose.

"What happened? Are you okay?" she asked with a concerned tinged voice.

"Yeah, I just needed to sleep it off," he said, brushing away her concern.

Alana sat on his bed and patted the place next to her. Kai sat down next to her and stared at the wall.

"I don't have a good relationship with my folks, Kai. In fact, it's non-existent".

Kai startled by the admission turned to face her.

"I know it doesn't look like it, but I am rich. And that comes with its own set of baggage. My parent's marriage was a business deal and there's no love lost between them. They performed their duty by producing my brother, who is the heir and me, the spare. Then they went about their lives like we didn't exist. Between nannies, boarding school, and putting up appearances, we both grew up."

"I'm sorry, I didn't know."

"How could you have? I don't publicize it. They fucked us up good, in different ways of course. I went through a dark phase when I was 15. I still hadn't realized the futility of trying to make my parents love me. I tried to get their attention by doing some questionable things. But it didn't make any difference. They threw their money at it to make it disappear. I had to get away from that toxic environment before it turned me insane or worse turned me into one of them."

She paused, catching her bearing.

"I waited till my trust fund kicked in, packed my bag and left without a word. Though I am not physically present there, mentally I still have scars that I'll carry for the rest of my life."

Kai sat there, not knowing what to say.

"Do you know why I decided to tell you about my past?" she asked.

Kai shook his head.

"There are days when my past overshadows my present. I can't put on a smile for myself, let alone the world. It changes you to know that your family doesn't love you, makes you think if you're even worthy of love. But I promised myself that I would never let them win and I work towards it every day."

Kai shook his head in dissent.

"And I might be wrong, but I think things are weighing you down too. Only you can help yourself and life is short Kai. But it's worth fighting for and I hope you do."

Kai stared at her, wishing he could say something to make her feel better. Then he surprised himself by pulling her into him and holding her.

"Thank you!" he whispered. Not knowing if he was thanking her for sharing her past or for recognizing that he was struggling.

Alana just tightened her arms.

"I want to say something. I know this is not the right time, but I need to get it out." he said nervously.

"What is it?"

They separated and Kai kept his eyes on the floor, unable to look at her.

"I like it. As more than a friend. I think I have always had a crush on you but this past month getting to know you made me like you even more." he confessed.

Alana just stared at her shoes, not saying anything. After what seemed like an eternity to Kai but was really a few minutes, she sighed and said "Kai…"

And Kai knew. He had taken a risk and now he was going to lose her.

"I'm sorry. I like you as a friend and nothing more. I apologize if I led you on in any way. That was never my intention. Besides, I have a boyfriend!" she said apologetically.

"What?" Kai asked sounding more surprised than devastated.

"He's a senior and we've been going out for a year. He's on an exchange program in Brazil right now."

Kai felt like he had been kicked in his chest. He felt betrayed and maybe he did have her figured out. She did know how to pull the rug out from under him.

"How is it that you never mentioned him before?" asked Kai, feeling hurt.

"It never came up," said Alana.

She continued, "I'm sorry Kai. I don't want to sound like a cliché, but I do hope we can stay friends. I mean it."

Kai replied, "Sure." But they both knew he didn't mean it.

Alana got up and left with a last beseeching glance at Kai. And Kai sat there, questioning how every time his life got even a little better, his happiness was snatched from him. Like someone up there couldn't stand to see him happy.

I always wondered, if knowing and losing was better than not knowing at all. Isn't ignorance bliss? It was probably one of the toughest moments in Kai's life. He slept most day, not even Mama Duong's berating could get him out of his bed. He felt like a zombie, incapable of thinking and feeling anything beyond his immediate needs. His parents were worried, not knowing how to help their son, unaware that they're part of the problem as well. 'Higher the climb, harder you fall' and Kai was still smarting from his fall. Nothing is crueller than fledgling hope stomped out before it could flourish.

*　　*　　*

We, humans, are social beings, we gravitate towards other people for companionship. We build ourselves a community and construct a society to be a part of. We obey the tenants set forth to remain a part of this said community. We feel a responsibility towards our immediate kin, their happiness, and their welfare. And we try to fit in with the larger society because that is what is expected of us. And before we know it, we're bogged down by expectations, guilt, and our need to be accepted. And we forget ourselves along the way, our individuality homogenized, our voices silenced and our wishes, a forgotten dream. We get through life like it's a chore, forgetting the magic of it. But some people are dreamers. Like Alana and Ayra. They struggle against the confines and limitations set by others, yearning to make their own rules and unfurl their wings. There will come a tipping point in one's life to choose. To subjugate or to break free. And if I am being honest, it is easier to choose the former. However heroic breaking free sounds, it would be the most painful experience you'd have to go through. Imagine breaking your bones to slip through the slits of the cage. A transformation that requires grit and unflinching determination to carry on.

Kai was at the tipping point of his life. He had reached his limit. Alana not returning his feelings wasn't the devastating blow, it was one among the series of many. In fact, it was the lynchpin that set off the dominos, the final push he needed to wake up from his long slumber. He had to choose himself for once and that began with having three conversations.

His parents were in the living room watching television when Kai interrupted them.

"Can I talk to you guys for a second?" asked Kai.

His Dad switched off the TV and focused on him.

"I know you guys think I am irresponsible and that I don't take my future seriously enough. And that I don't measure up to Hanh." he started.

His mother interrupted him before he could continue.

"Kai, we don't think that." Mama Duong denied.

"Let me say my piece and you can give your opinion later on. You guys haven't said it in so many ways but it's the way you've made me feel."

"And how is that our fault Kai? If you assume things, how can we be held responsible?" admonished his Dad.

"Dad, please you're making this hard. Do you have any idea how unhappy I have been for the past few years? I am living a lie, Dad. I am living a life created for me by you. And I am stuck. I am tired of trying to make you happy and failing. I am being pulled in two different directions. Why do you think I sleep so much? Not because I am lazy, but because it's painful to be awake. I've been distancing myself from my friends because I am ashamed. Ashamed of who I have become, I am terrified that they'd pity me. I want to live my life for myself from now and I want to make myself happy." Kai confessed, pouring out years worth of anguish and resentment.

His parents remained silent and his Dad asked finally,

"And how do you plan on doing that?"

"Once I graduate, I am going to art school," he said with a finality that he hadn't believed in until that moment.

"And what do you think Kai? You can make a living as an artist?" sneered Papa Duong.

"I don't care Dad. I am dying slowly in the life you've chosen for me. I'd rather make my own decisions and fail at them than have regrets later. At least it would have been my decision."

"You sound like the child you are Kai. Do you think we came to this country and worked so hard to throw away your life like this? I am not going to pay for art school, you can be sure of that!" said Papa Duong indignantly.

"I don't expect you to be happy with my decision, but I do want you to respect it. And no, you don't have to pay for it, I'm going to apply for scholarships".

With that, he left his parents. His mother's grief-stricken face and his Dad's fury deeply etched in his mind.

The next conversation he had was with Ayra. This went better than the previous conversation. He knew he couldn't do it alone and he needed people in his corner. He apologized for being a shitty friend over the years and told her the truth, about the things he wasn't ready to face then. He vowed to be a better friend to her and the gracious friend that she was, she accepted his apology.

The last conversation he had was with himself. And that came with its own trials and tribulations. It was painful for him to accept who he had become, to confront himself. He knew he hadn't been living and that he had just been merely existing. He knew it but he didn't "KNOW" it. It is one of those things that you have always been aware of, but you weren't ready to acknowledge it yet. He wanted to focus on himself now, even if that meant disappointing his parents. It hurt him greatly to do so but it was time he put himself first. He had been floating, lost in the sea, when unexpectedly he was given a life vest. He still didn't know if he could be friends with Alana, but he was thankful she had come into his life. Through the short period that he had known her, he realized that he had the capacity to be happy. We meet a lot of people in our lives, not everyone is meant to stay but without fail, they all leave a mark on you. Life is hard, it is terrifying to face it. He knew he had to make changes in his life. Kai knew he had to get help; he had already booked an appointment with the University counsellor. It was not an easy path, there will be days when the shadows would hound him, when he wouldn't make it out of his bed, when everything in the world would work against him. But that's alright because now he knew there would be better days as well. He had to be his own saviour and it was a tough lesson to learn. It was two years in the making, but now he knew he couldn't wait for anyone else to change his life. He had to don his armour and slay the dragon, not to save the princess but to save himself. I told you it wasn't going to be a happy ending, at least not the one you expected. In our brokenness, we find ourselves, and this was the beginning of Kai.

HOW ARE YOU DOING TODAY?

WRITE 3 GOOD THINGS THAT HAPPENED WITH

YOU IN YOUR DAY.

3

The Mind Grind

By Sanyogita Bharadwaj

◆◇◆

It was a breezy morning; it was after almost 6 months Aisha had woken up and saw the sunrise. She was in the final stage of her journey.

July 10th, 2017

"I just can't do this anymore, this is not happening, I always failed. I don't want to fail now. I want this to be a successful end." said Aisha sitting on the floor running out of breath with a bottle full of sleeping pills.

Yathrath holds her with all his might trying to get her off the sleeping pills. "This phase will go. This will be over, trust me please Aisha." said Yatharth. "Aisha, breathe! Slowly."

Aisha slowly let her grip loose on the sleeping pills and collapsed.

It's just another morning where Yathrath slides the curtain and lets Aisha sleep a little more. He looked at her. Kind of lost in thoughts and partly in her. He remembers the girl he saw while they were young kids. Her smile was brighter than the first to eat the day of the Sun. She was the synonym of joy.

Aisha was abused as a child by her father physically and mentally. She lost her mother two years ago, since then Aisha stayed in Hyderabad with her family friends who were more like family. Yathrath was their son. Before her mother's death, she fell for Kabir. A classic fuckboy who decided to use her emotionally vulnerable self as a pathway to his bed. What could amuse one the most was, he chose to put her through all of it despite knowing what she had been fighting with. After two years of emotional abuse, Aisha called quits. But doing that she did not realize if she was punishing herself or him, it was indeed herself. Her mother's death came like another storm amidst all this. Now panic attacks and depression had become a very toxic part of her everyday life. One day Yathrath had found her standing over the edge of the terrace with sleepless and tear-drenched eyes. He immediately got her off. That was the day when Yathrath noticed how vulnerable and unstable she was.

Yatharth had just come from his morning jog. He looks for his shirt in the closet. He suddenly hears cries. Numb cries with heavy breathing. "Aisha?" he knocked the door. "Aisha are you there?" on not getting a response he slowly unlocked the door. He saw Aisha on the bed. Sweating profusely, grabbing sheets, weeping, repeatedly whispering "Save me" going through a nightmare. He falls short of words on seeing that. He sprinkles water on her face, and she gains consciousness. "Aisha? You okay?" asked Yatharth. "He…. he will kill me. I will bump into him someday and he will kill me. Do you know? He called me a whore and…. And you know he hit me blue and black. Save me please." said Aisha. Scared clinging on to his arm and shivering she muttered "Will he come again?"

"No one will come. Nothing will happen. I promise you Aisha." Said Yatharth and Aisha calmed down. Slowly and steadily. Yatharth held her assuring nothing would happen. Her father would never get a chance to show his power on her. Yes, he couldn't. But the impact he had left lasted longer than the abuse done. Aisha often woke up to nightmares. It had become a part of her life. Yatharth noticed that he's seen Aisha on the same clothes for 2 days now. She stayed in bed all day long. Yatharth's parents would insist her to join them for dinner but she'd kindly refuse or lie that she ate already. She'd lay in bed all day long. At times crying, at times staring at the ceiling and at times sleeping. She'd try her best and skip meals. She grew skinny with every passing day. She had begun stress sleeping to avoid her thoughts, the overthinking, and the endless battles her mind manipulated and expected her to fight. She wouldn't take shower at times. She'd not dress up or even do her hair. She lost the desire to live. Suicidal thoughts were like terrorists that invaded her mind which Yatharth's efforts fought like soldiers.

"Aisha, go take a shower. See you at the breakfast table?"

"No Yatharth. Sorry. I can't. I don't want to. Thanks for calming this chaos I caused though."

"Thank me by taking a shower. And maybe on the breakfast table here? Don't say no." said Yatharth.

"Umm okay," says Aisha weakly with a smile.

Yatharth arranged breakfast while Aisha gets done with a shower.

"What's up dude?" said Aisha. "Nothing much I just thought I'll put a pretty bed sheet for this pretty girl," said Yatharth.

"Weird," said Aisha and sits down for breakfast. She fidgets with the spoon, staring at the ceiling.

"Aisha"

"Yeah?"

"I'd love to see your brilliance in culinary skills but later. We'll eat for now. Okay?"

"Okay," said Aisha.

"Aisha, I want you to see a Therapist," said Yatharth

Are you kidding me? Do you think I'm crazy? Like those people in mental asylums?"

"Did I say that? I didn't say anything like that Aisha."

"Then what do you mean? Tell me? Tell me Yatharth tell me right now, what did you mean?" almost yelled Aisha

"You're unstable. You aren't mad. Listen carefully, you know Aisha? You could carry two bags from the mart or maybe three. I'll handover you the fourth one. You'll still walk but now at a slow pace. I'll give you another bag and you will fail to carry it any further. You'll stumble and fall. You'll try to get up but will fail because it's too heavy. You'll stop and not walk. But what if I help? We could divide the baggage. Leave the bags in their place one by one and set ourselves free at once. In the same way, after everything life has thrown towards you, you're walking with this unnecessary baggage. No sorry, you were. And now you're at a standstill. A therapist will let you leave that baggage in the right places. You will be happy again, trust me. If not happy, you'll not be sad. Try to understand, I'm not blaming you neither am I saying that you're mad. I'm saying, let's see a therapist. I want you to live once again. Please? I'll come with you; I'll be there for you I promise." said Yatharth.

"Umm okay, but one condition," said Aisha.

"Yeah?" asked Yatharth.

"You will accompany me for every therapy session. I'm not comfortable. I honestly don't wish to go out. But you're insisting so." said Aisha.

"I will, I promise," said Yatharth.

That evening Yatharth and Aisha were on their way to the hospital. Yatharth took an appointment and Aisha sat rubbing her hands anxiously.

"Aye, chill Aisha. We're here for help. You will not fall from one pit to another. Don't let your hopes die." said Yatharth.

"I hope so," said Aisha and spends two hours looking around.

"Aisha Krishnan next," said the nurse.

Aisha nervously gets up, begins with slow steps towards the doctor's cabin and smiles weakly at Yatharth while he gestures all the best. Aisha walked in and wished Dr. Aravind a good evening. They exchange smiles. Dr. Aravind had been fifteen minutes in conversation asking Aisha regarding her hobbies and dreams. He slowly did make Aisha loosen up a bit.

"So, tell me, Aisha, I want you to put your entire life before me. Place trust in me. I know it's difficult. Have faith in me and trust me. We'll do it. But let's take baby steps. Begin with your childhood." said Dr. Aravind.

Aisha's eyes fill up with tears. She chokes with a heavy lump of sorrow in her throat. She stammers, "I…."

"Yes Aisha, I'm listening. I'm here. I'll be there. For you. Tell me." said Dr. Aravind.

"Will you reveal this to him? I mean Yatharth. He knows most of it but not in detail." said Aisha.

"Don't worry. I can't even if you want me to. I have no right to do so till you indicate chances of self-harm or harming others. So, don't worry about that." said Dr. Aravind.

The next 30 minutes seemed to be Aisha's most difficult 30 minutes. She cried, went gibberish in tears and smiled weakly a few times. Dr. Aravind listened to all of it, sought permission and called for Yatharth.

After three more sessions in the presence of Yatharth, Dr. Aravind said "Clinical Depression. But you know? If you were brave enough to tell me everything, you're brave enough to leave this put. Yatharth, I might not be there at all times. I hope you will when I can't. And Aisha, we will do this together and shock even your demons. I promise."

Yatharth and Aisha leave with a smile. They know the tough journey has begun. But they also knew the destination was worth the struggle. But Aisha was confused if she could withstand this journey.

Aisha didn't utter a word on the way back home. Yatharth stayed mum to thinking she might just want to slowly quit recalling those memories. They stop by a restaurant to eat. Aisha doesn't talk for quite some time now.

"Aisha? You okay?" asked Yatharth. "Absolutely fine," replied Aisha with a forced smile.
They drive home and Aisha says she's very tired, needs rest and disappears in the room. It's 04:00 am. Yatharth wakes up to quench his thirst and notices that Aisha's rooms still have their lights on. He thinks of checking on her but feels to let the calm remain. Little did he know, it was the calm before the storm.

3 Days later,

"Aisha? Aishaaaa? Aisha opens the door Shikha has come here to see you. She's been waiting for more than 20 minutes. Open the door or just respond." yelled Yatharth

"I'm sorry. She just isn't responding. Did you call her up before starting?" asked Yatharth.

"I'm afraid but I think it's too late," said Shikha.

"Huh? What? What are you saying? What are you talking about?" Yatharth began to panic.

"Didn't she tell you?" asked Shikha.

"Tell me what is it? No riddles right now. Tell me damnit!" says Yatharth in a tone no one ever heard him speaking in. He'd been sweating and stood with his hands buried in his palms for a moment and ran upstairs. Shikha follows. "Aisha! Open the door. Just open the door!" yelled Yatharth.

"She left I guess," said Shikha. "What? Left? Where? When? Tell me Shikha please." said Yatharth. "She was planning to leave the town," said Shikha in the lowest tone possible.

Yatharth kicks open Aisha's door in frustration. He enters her room opens the cupboards, sees through her books, and finally finds a note. Almost crumbled.

Hi. What's up? How annoyed are you? See this is what I do. I don't smile. At times I take away smiles too. I guess it's time I leave. I do not know if I'll come back though. Or I even might but all I know is that I don't want to be your burden anymore. I don't want to worry you anymore. This is my life. My journey. My problem. I think it's time you take lead in your own life rather than mine. Don't panic if you don't ever find me. Don't worry even as you're reading this. I'm left with no desire.

Maybe this is my end. Maybe this is where you have to finish writing my story and begin a new one. Smile and get back to work. Forget me and my nonsense.

Love.

Aisha.

Yatharth's eyes fill up with tears. He crumbled the letter and began to sob. "You aren't my damn headache Aisha you're whole of my heart," said Yatharth sobbing uncontrollably.
Shikha laid her hand on Yatharth's shoulder. "I understand how you feel right now. Any friend would feel the same," said Shikha. Yatharth gave her a death stare.

"Only if you had given me some hint this wouldn't happen. You knew what was going on in her head. Just one hint. Now if you're done with this hide and seek, she's made you a part of, kindly help me in locating her. She's not in a mental state where she can be left on her own. Please, I beg you Shikha." Said Yatharth.

"See, don't panic. She left last night and would either meet Azra or her aunt is what I know. She wouldn't go back to Bangalore because of Kabir. Vizag or Mumbai is my guess." Said Shikha.

Yatharth tries texting her on all her social media accounts. Tried calling but in vain as her phone says out of coverage area. He imagines the most dreaded possibilities in his head. She could again attempt a long jump. Swallow sleeping pills. The very thought of something like that itself made sweat beads escape his forehead. He randomly opens the map on Snapchat.

'Trisha Krishnan. Dombivali. 4 hours ago.' says her location on the map. He smiled in relief and sighed.

"Phew. Thank God. She's in Mumbai. I'll have to leave. Anyway, thank you for helping me out. Please keep in touch as I might need help." Said Yatharth.

"Sure. Bye," said Shikha.

Yatharth sets out for Mumbai with no real clue where could Aisha be. He hires an auto to reach the hotel.

"Auto! Auto! Rukjao bhi Bhaiya!" said a familiar voice and a young woman takes a seat next to him and takes off her scarf.

"WHAT THE FUCK?" they both yelled at once. The young woman was none other than Aisha.

"How on earth do you think you can disappear? Are you out of your mind Aisha?" yelled Yatharth holding her by her shoulders.

"Yes, Yatharth. I'm out of mind. That's what I was trying to explain to you. I'm glad you understood." said Aisha breaking down into soft sobs. Yatharth held his face in his palms.

"Aisha you aren't my burden. Why are you running away? Till, when will you? I told you we're in this together. I promised to stay and even come for every therapy session. You can't leave midway. Please." said Yatharth.

After hours of talking Yatharth figured out that the breakdown she had before Dr. Aravind contributed to all this with a stupid phone call from Kabir. The conversation with Dr. Aravind had brought back many memories that had partly healed and hadn't healed at all. Her anxiety played tricks on her mind saying what if this throws you the deeper pit of depression and got her running around leaving everything behind. But we all need a little motivation to face our fears. Yatharth became a source. We all need a little initial push to run towards things and get over them. Dr. Aravind had pledged to become that push.

"Yatharth."

"Yeah?" said Yatharth.

"What do I do with Kabir? Am I being unjust to him? Am I being a bad person? Should I take him back?" asked Aisha. Yatharth held her hand in his, knelt down and said, "See, you don't need toxic people back in your life. Some people never realize or change. It's not like I'm shitting you. You gave him a second chance and you know better." said Yatharth.

"I do but,"

"No ifs and buts Aisha. We're going back. And I'm not letting the shadows of yesterday haunt you," said Yatharth.
She blocked Kabir everywhere possible.

"How did you know that I'd be here though?" asked Aisha.

"I sent a detective behind you," said Yatharth with a smirk.

"For once will you shut up and get out of your just kidding mode?" said Aisha and Yatharth hummed a song-

"Hain nahi tha pata, ki tujhe maanluga khuda ki teri galliyon mein iss kadar aaunga ab har peher." and smiled.

"You wanna sing anything more Galliyaan or something? Please do but first answer me," frowned Aisha.

"See, you're very smart and all but very forgetful," smirked Yatharth.

"Eh? Tell now," pleaded Aisha.

"Snapchat location and a friend of yours. Like my co-detective you see," said Yatharth and laughed out.

"Damn," said Aisha and smiles in surprise.

The next day, they packed up and started for the airport to board the next flight to Hyderabad. They got down the taxi. Aisha waited to hold her bag and Yatharth paid the driver. Meanwhile, a Scorpio came racing towards Yatharth.

"Yathaaaaaaarrrthh!!! Watch out!!" yelled Aisha and ran towards him and pulled him aside. They both stood panting. Yatharth smiled at her. "Are you bloody mad? Are you blind? What would I do if something happened to you? What would I answer if Uncle and aunty asked?" yelled Aisha.

"Now you know where I stood. Did you think for once what would I answer myself? You also are as precious as I'm. To mum, dad, me and this world," said Yatharth.

They get back to Hyderabad. Yatharth separately convinces her to continue therapy. She promises not to run away this time. Yatharth's parents stand with her too. Her knowing that she wasn't alone was enough for her this time. Aisha now was ready to see Dr. Aravind. She now had enough strength to accept and let go of the past. Her attacks hadn't left yet but now even she had decided to not give up no matter how tough things went. Cut to Therapy. Aisha now told what bothers her. She stammers at times before Dr. Aravind but eventually gets the flow. She now becomes comfortably vulnerable. Dr. Aravind had now become like a father figure to the little girl longing for love within her. Anti-depressants made sure she slept well. Her stress was slowly fading away. The progress was slow, but she definitely was coming back to normal. When told about Kabir's attempt to come back Dr. Aravind shook his head.

"Bacha, now that we've come this far, you'll not give up okay. We're at this critical point where one step back will take you to square one. And one step ahead will make sure you don't look back." said Dr. Aravind.

*　　　*　　　*

Life was getting better for good. Dr. Arvind stayed throughout the panic attacks, the depression that had sworn not to leave, the slit wrists and the violent sobs backed by Yathrath.

There were days Aisha did not want to eat, she'd go into a panic mode and start throwing anything that came her way.

Yathrath would hold her with all his love and patience. He would miss work at times just to shoo Aisha's demons away from her. There were days she'd refuse therapy but eventually came. It took her all the love from Yatharth and a lot of patience and dedication from Dr. Arvind to get over the abuse she was put through by two men who were supposed to love her to death. She was a depression survivor. A brave one, and braver were these two men to hold her and stand by her unshook throughout. Aisha's depression was a battle she was scared to fight. But once the warrior within her rose up she conquered all the battles. With each therapy session, there were minute changes taking place. After one she'd smile, after another one talk like a chirpy bird, weak smiles into healthy laughter, avoiding food was rare and above everything she was learning to rise and live. She'd now have a sound sleep. Anti-depressants and therapy sessions were all working fine. Another mile and they'd reach the destination anytime. Aisha would start Living again. With the desire, without fear.

December 2nd, 2017

"So? Tell me, Aisha, how has it been? How different is it?" asked Dr. Arvind.

Aisha took a deep breath and smiled. She didn't have words to describe it. She felt good about herself & life for the first time in years.

"Feels like a rebirth Doc, I don't know how else to explain."

"I know your anti-depressant dose stops today. I know this is your last day here. As much as I'd miss seeing this strong woman blossoming into a warrior, I'm glad we waged a war and conquered your demons together."

There's a pause…

"You're one of the strongest patients I've known, you're someone I'm really proud of, you're my achievement as a therapist," said Dr. Aravind.

January 28th, 2018

"Hello, where are you? I've been waiting for 30mins straight in this cafe. I'm all awkward!" said Aisha.

"I'm leaving if you don't show up in ten." said Aisha.

"Arey! Ten okay just ten minutes I promise," said Yatharth

"Okay." Said Aisha and hung up.

Yathrath comes with a huge cake hiding his face with a gorgeous bouquet of roses. Aisha was overwhelmed. Yathrath looks at Aisha and says, "I know and will always know that you will win over every battle of life no matter what."

"Not alone though," said Aisha.

"Then? Dr. Aravind?" asks Yatharth.

"You," she said and stuffed a piece of the cake she just cut in Yatharth's mouth.

"Let's celebrate this victory, your victory over this battle and your victory over this heart of mine!" said Yathrath with a flashing smile. They both blushed like idiots and confessed love.

*   *   *

Aisha is a prompt example that most of us suffer from day to day battles, cry ourselves to sleep and are suicidal at times. Also, that one is stronger than his/her depression or any mental battle and can survive and conquer it. Also, seeking help from a loved one or opting for therapy is not something to be ashamed of. As friends and loved ones, it is also our duty to check on our loved ones. Yathrath and Dr. Aravind are prompt examples that therapy or at most love and affection is just what one needs in dark times. I promise to support every loved one, so should you. You being there could save a life. Be there for someone and let someone be there when you need to. Embracing your emotions, remaining vulnerable and stepping over things that once stepped on you is the bravest thing you can do. Do not shy away from help. Letting you know that you're stronger than your problems, those break downs, higher than your lows and at most a beautiful soul the world needs. I take your leave.

WRITE YOUR NEGATIVE THOUGHTS IN THE BOTTLE IN THE LOCK IT UP FOREVER AND WHEN YOU DO THAT WRITE HOW ARE YOU FEELING AFTER DOING THAT IN THE GLASS NEXT TO IT.

4

BON VOYAGE

By Kanika Choudhary

Let's go back to those fairy tales, let's relive that naive childhood
Sometimes our mind doesn't want to accept certain situations
and therefore we keep trying to run away from them, but let's
face it, we have to face them. Maybe not now, but in the future,
we sure have to.

12.12.2018
Dear diary,

Today I want to share and talk to you about something
that I have never talked about. It's a tale about self-discovery and
self-analyzation. I will try to keep it short and crisp. This is
something that I like to remind myself time and again, that no
matter how difficult life gets, you circle back to it, so just keep

taking deep breaths and do one day at a time and you will be just fine.

So here it goes:

Meera Kapoor was a simple high school girl. Her parents shifted to London before she was born. She was someone who liked the occasional clubbing and was incredibly open about life. Her world revolved around her friends, but she always used to over-analyze situations and worried about things that weren't even there. Just like how every girl dreamt about her first love and first kiss to be perfect, she always dreamt of how it would feel and how this word "LOVE" could be so magical.

Meera had a perfect group of friends, a straight-out-of-a-movie type of group, who would pull each other's legs for no good reason or just abused each other without giving a damn about the formalities. She would always tell her friends that she believed in love but the idea of completing another person's life, she never understood. She always wondered how someone could complete a whole another human.

But little did she know her whole world was about to turn.

It all began with the "senior prom". Meera, as usual, being the most enthusiastic one was ready an hour early and started with her patent anthem of, "Hurry up fools, we're going to be late", but there was a reason why Luv was late today.

**Ok ok so quick reel back!

LUV KAPOOR was Meera's twin brother and the most in-demand and famous boy in school. The twins had half of the crowd head over heels for them, but they were too naive to notice that. **

The Doorbell rang

"Hey, Meera could you get that please?" Luv shouted.

Meera opened the door.

And there he was, KABIR DUTT.

Ok ok, that's it for today. I will tell you more about Kabir tomorrow.

Love, xoxo

13.12.2018

Dear diary,

Kabir Dutt was Meera's crush since junior high but she had never gathered the courage to talk to him. They always shared looks in the hallway, but it never went beyond that. Kabir was in the basketball team and was popular for his three-pointer shots. The level of madness he would create during his game was unbelievable

"Hey, Kabir! You are here, come on in!" Meera's dad greeted Kabir with excitement.

"So, as I see, you are here to take Meera for the prom?" Meera's dad continued.

Meera gave her father an embarrassed look.

"Yes, sir! I am here to take Meera to the prom." Kabir replied.

"WHAT?" Meera shouted!

"Oh, there it is, SURPRISE!" Luv shouted with happiness.

It all seemed so surreal for Meera.

"Hey! Hold on, can someone tell me what's going on here? And Kabir since when are 'we' going together for prom?" Confused, Meera questioned.

"Meera, I know you! I am your twin, remember? Now come on, stop analyzing it and have an amazing last prom." Luv nudged and urged her to go.

So yeah, I guess good things do happen when you least expect them too.

Kabir escorts Meera to his car "So I guess this is how it all starts. On prom. I guess it is the perfect day." Kabir whispered.

For Meera, it all seemed like a dream. There was a whole bunch of dinosaurs running in her tummy. That tingling feeling of shyness and excitement all together.

"Ooh, Lala! That is one sexy car!" Meera exclaimed.

Kabir like a gentleman opened the car door for Meera.

Kabir had always been fond of cars, and his dad is one of the richest & reputed businessmen in town, always fulfilled his desires.

"Yes, it sure is" Kabir smiled and replied.

"Hey, you can connect your phone to the car Bluetooth and play your music?" he asked.

"Let's see your taste in music" he flirted

"My taste in music is amazing, ok? I hope you do like it though." Meera replied.

Meera connected her phone via Bluetooth and played her all-time favourite song.

Thinking Out Loud plays

"Wow, you sure have got a crazy playlist Meera," he mentioned

"So, tell me something about you MK". I hope you don't mind me calling you MK?" he questioned.

"No, that actually is the coolest name someone has ever given me, I like it." Meera blushed and replied.

Hey, diary don't you think they looked adorable together. I think so too. I will tell you more gossip later.

Got to go!

Bye.

Love,

xoxo.

14.12.2018

Dear diary,

I guess the senior prom did bring Meera showers of confetti and glitters. After the prom, the chemistry between the two had just exploded. Meera was ecstatic by the idea of having a boyfriend. She had never thought of dating earlier, and especially dating Kabir was definitely not on the plan, but as it is said: "whatever happens, happens for a reason". And so, the bud of love bloomed after that. The two were inseparable. From sneaking around at night to lunch dates, they did it all. They would go to amusement parks, coffee breaks and would never leave an opportunity to sneak in each other's houses. They were adorable. Kabir had this weirdly cute smile that Meera would melt for. Kabir wasn't the most expressive one but Meera always knew that, and never had an expectation for anything extraordinary. But at the end of the day she was a girl, she had always wanted someone who would pamper her with gifts, chocolates, and flowers. The relationship between Meera and Kabir was a little different from other couples. They didn't have any drama or formalities. Or let's just say they didn't like to play the blame game of who called whom first. This was so different from what Meera had in her mind, but this was something that she never wanted to let go of. She was having the time of her life, or at least she thought it to be.

Meera was someone who liked to pamper people that she loved, it was her kick to pamper her friends and family, and now Kabir was on the list too. Again, Kabir wasn't the most expressive guy and whenever Meera took an extra step for him and did something for him, she expected a good reply, which actually is human nature. We don't expect people to go lengths for us all the time, but at least seek appreciation at some point of time.

A few weeks down the line, Kabir got the most exciting news. He had gotten his college scholarship.

"Hey, Meera! Meera I got it; I got the scholarship!" Kabir shouted

"Oh my god! That is so amazing, Kabir! I am so happy for you!" Meera replied.

But was she really happy with this news? Her dreams were different from Kabir's and she subconsciously had known that this would end at some point of time. She just didn't want that time to be now.

But sometimes good things have an expiration date too, and after a while, it all seemed to be breaking apart. Meera was so indulged in her fairy tale love story, that she couldn't see the changes in Kabir's behaviour as time passed. There were missed lunches, cancelled plans, and let's not forget even the missing of her birthday.

At first, she was heartbroken by Kabir not having immediately wished her on her birthday, but then she thought that he would have planned a surprise for her. Sadly, that wasn't the case though. Kabir was so busy trying to flaunt his scholarship that he forgot her birthday. It wasn't even on his mind. She confronted him and the reply only disappointed her.

She knew it wouldn't last anymore; the fairy tale romance was in its last chapter.

The sudden break up shattered Meera into a million pieces. But somewhere it felt like the breakup wasn't sudden, it was just the realization that came suddenly. Luv being a brother and having a protective side for his sister, questioned Kabir about his sudden move. After being continually questioned, Kabir had only one answer, "I don't know, I don't feel the same anymore."

No no no, I can't talk about it anymore.

Too many flashbacks.

Sorry.

Bye diary.

Love,

xoxo.

15.12.2018

Dear diary,

Luv had blamed himself for all the mess as he had played the role of cupid in Meera and Kabir's love story. Somewhere, he felt responsible for Meera's depression.

Meera didn't even want to step outside of her room. She would spend hours and days in the room just scribbling in her diary. After a while, she even stopped talking to Luv. She just wanted to be alone. Luv tried his best to take her out for carnivals and movies, but she was too afraid to go outside and even face the idea of Kabir being around.

Meera's worst traits were that she never wanted to face things and always ran away from these kinds of situations. During this phase, she found an interesting way to run away from her problems. She wanted to get lost in Italy. Italy was one of the places that she had always wanted to go to. The idea of Italy would always calm her, so this time when she was struggling the most, all she could think about was going to Italy. With no connections and no solid plan. As graduation was around the corner, the timing seemed pretty perfect for her. She wanted to get lost, get lost in the crowd with the hope of finding herself again, where no one knew her or would judge her. She knew this was the only way she would find herself again and would finally be able to look herself in the mirror with confidence and pride.

The impact of Meera's impromptu decision came as a shock to her family. She decided to take a gap year. This was a shock as Meera had been accepted to Harvard for her further studies and going to Italy would put her admission on stake. At this point, Meera wanted to put her mental health first and wanted to get out of this state of mind and she knew to stay in the same city as Kabir would be difficult at this point of time. She wanted her parents to believe in her and support her in this situation and that was what they did.

Meera- "Mom. Dad. Luv. I want to talk to you guys about something. As you know, things didn't work between me and Kabir. I wish I could have done something to convince him to stay with me a little longer, but I failed, I failed miserably, and I know I have disappointed you both and Luv. But believe me, I am trying. I am trying really, hard, but I can't do it anymore. No matter where I go, may it be school or the park across the town, it just reminds me of him. I feel like an idiot who has no idea about her life. I need to get my act together."

Meera's mother- "Oh honey! Come here. You have not disappointed anyone. Your dad and I could not be prouder of you. Do you know what your biggest strength is? It's that you know what is wrong with you, and you want to get out of it. Not many people have that in them. Your dad and I are always going to be with you.

Luv interrupted- "Umm me too Meera. I am your twin, and as mom says, I came 5 mins before you, so that technically makes me older than you. And as your older brother I can proudly say that you are strong; so, so strong. Even though you can't pick up a 2 kg weight in the gym.

Everyone giggles

Meera' dad- "I see a smile. There it is, there it is."

Everyone starts tickling Meera

Meera's dad- "Ok, I promise you, ask me anything right now and I promise to give it to you sweetheart! Remember, no boy is worth your tears. I love you, honey!"

Meera presented her idea and was just hoping to get a yes from her parents. As a parent, it definitely disturbs you with the idea of sending away your child to an unknown country. But seeing Meera in depression her parents wanted to do what was best for her and finally decided to send Meera to Italy on two conditions.

Only if Harvard accepts to push the admission for the next year (so that they have back up) and;

If Luv agrees to do his culinary course for 6 months from Italy (which basically was Luv's dream)

Meera knew it wouldn't be easy to just go away, but she wanted to surround herself with different cultures and wanted to get find her true self again, not only her school and what she really wanted to pursue.

I will tell you about Italy in my next entry and I promise to keep it short.

Bye!

Love,

xoxo.

16.12.2018

Dear diary,

Italy was like a dream for Luv, he always wanted to go to Italy and work with some amazing chefs and find his own flavour. Luv knew this would be good for Meera and him both.

They decided to explore Italy together, no matter how busy they would get with their own work they promised to sit down for dinner every day together and talk about each other's day. As it is said, life gets easy when you have someone to share your happiness and sorrows. A simple question "How was your day?" can sometimes make you think about all the incidents that happened in the day and you are recalling it with your loved ones, you tend to think that your day wasn't that bad also. The first thing on their crazy list was to learn Italian and that's what they did, they went to the old school, they started to pick up the phrase from different cafes and surprisingly people were good to them. Strangers taught them some simple phrases that they could use to communicate.

This was all very thrilling for Meera. This is what she wanted. This is what she came for. To find herself, to find her identity.

Italy treated them well. Luckily, Luv got this amazing internship with an Italian chef and Meera met an amazing group of travellers from Austria. It was like a cultural exchange for her. She not only got to know about their culture but also learned so much more about different counties and the most important about life. She knew a guy couldn't control her happiness anymore. She explored herself, she got to know herself much better now. This trip did change Luv & Meera's perspective about life and both became clear about what they want in life.

So, this was my version of their journey I really hope one day I become as strong as Meera and don't let stupid boys ruin my future behind them. This all for now. I got to go, have school tomorrow.

Bye

Love xoxo.

DRAW YOUR FAVORITE FRUIT AND WRITE HOW YOU FEEL WHILE EATING IT.

5

A Combat with My Compadres

By Sree Yelamanchi

— ◆◇◆ —

I grew up with a friend who stuck with me through day and night. She was like my silhouette. She followed me everywhere. I didn't like her much, but she never ever left my side. Her voice was very captivating and then she would often cast this transfixing gaze which made me surrender to her every command. Whenever I tried to socialize, she would pull me back and I couldn't fight her brawniness. She would always come in my way of making friends. She was very clingy and possessive. Sometimes she fled when I am around a few people I love the most, when I am immensely secure and gleeful, maybe she felt intimidated in their presence, but she would return back judiciously every night. And this, her leaving my side would happen very occasionally.

I always used to end up brawling with her whenever I was invited to a party or had to attend a social gathering to let me go alone. But all in vain. If somehow, I fought my way through to go, she would reach there before me. She wouldn't let me talk to any new person. Sometimes it was as if she bewitched me and I suddenly had a blackout. She would always convince me to stay home, read a book or listen to music or watch my favourite TV show on repeat mode. She would persistently tell me that I am better off alone. And almost all the time I caved. Nobody could see the immense strength I needed to fight her back but never succeeded. Nobody could hear my shrill voice asking her to leave me alone. She would daunt me not to open up to anyone. She wouldn't allow me to pour my heart out to even my closest kin. I would hear her saying if I did so I will look stupid and people would laugh at me. I used to believe her naively. She was there always sitting right across me, whenever I was low or had a test to give or even when I had to talk to a stranger. She was my best companion all through my childhood, teenage and even my early 20's.

Then, one day, I met someone, a guy. My heart sensed a new feeling which felt straight out of a fairy tale. I was comfortable in my own skin around him. I giggled, I talked my heart out with no inhibitions, I was totally me when I was with him. I felt like a puzzle who suddenly found its long-lost missing piece. For the first time in my life, I trusted someone, I opened up to someone, I talked about every damn thing that popped up in my head. My heart and mind knew no bounds. It was new to me, to talk with no apprehensions, to love with no hesitancy and to believe with no fear in mind. I loved him more than I ever imagined. My life started feeling all new and different to me. It then flashed through my mind, that my friend was nowhere to be seen when he was around me. I felt relieved after years of battling with her. Whenever she tried to bother me, I used to hold his hand very tightly and she wouldn't dare to come near me. She would creep back occasionally when he was not around, but I was sure she would leave as he would come back to repel her. He was my new lifeline. Sometimes she would go missing for weeks and I wouldn't even acknowledge her absence. I was happy. I finally found out the perennial fix to my proprietorial friend. At least, I thought so.

A few years passed by with him by my side, with my ever-growing love towards him and of course, with my friend who would drop by once in a while. But kudos to her persistence and the way she incessantly tried coming back to me. Slowly, she started visiting me more often. I was terrified to admit her comeback. I was petrified of her haunting presence. I didn't want her back in my life. I knew if she comes back this time, there was no turning back for her. She came back every time when things heated up between us and with every visit, her stay was longer. I wanted him to go back to be that person who never judged me, who loved me for what I am. I wanted him to see the truth of the scheming minds around him tainting our lives. But my every effort to make him perceive the truth only paved way to my long-lost friend to come closer to me again. Whenever she did come close, I looked for him desperately, to hold his hand, to terrorize her with his presence but I used to fail in the quest miserably. He wouldn't be there almost all the time, and those few times when I used to find him, he wouldn't lend me his hand and rather would just shoo me away pushing me straight into her preying arms. Days went by and words started inflicting more pain than wounds, but I lingered on with a hope that better days were ahead, and he will eventually see the truth.

But he had different plans which I was oblivious to and which I never even thought of in my wildest dreams. And one day, to my horror, I woke up to her startling voice. She had a gleam in her eyes, and it was frightening to look at her. I knew that familiar gleam and that vicious smile of hers which she flashes when she wins. It struck me then that she was back for good. I started looking out for him frantically. She told me repeatedly that he left me for good, for acquisitive things, for few devious people and I had to heed her orders now. I didn't want to believe her though she was telling the truth, so I searched for him in all possible places I could but all I could find was bruises, agony, betrayal, and remains of dreams, hopes, and loyalty. I screamed imploring him to come back but he was nowhere to be seen. I was devastated. My life just came crashing down, my trust was stabbed into a sieve and I could feel my heart turning cold. In a whisk, my life turned topsy-turvy.

And, then there was a big surprise in her comeback this time. She was not alone. She brought her best friend to befriend me. I hated her. She was more overwhelming and surprisingly mightier than my childhood buddy. She was way more tenacious. Both of them were inseparable. Their words were so gripping that I was executing every order of their unerringly. They used to not let me out of my bed or eat for weeks. They constantly pestered me to stay awake until the wee hours of the morning and cry my heart out. Their voices were so demanding that it felt like someone was directly talking to my mind. They wouldn't even let me talk to my family. They would make me curse myself, question my worth and loathe my life. Sometimes they would perpetually tell me that I was a failure, I was not right for this world, should give up on life and have to end this pain once for all. I wanted to oblige them. I tried but I couldn't. I used to scream, plead, beg them to go away but they wouldn't even pay attention. I was a mere doll dancing to their tunes. I hated my life. I hated them.

One day after a long tough scuffle of months, I went out with my family, my people. These are the ones that love me for what I am. They are not like those name-sake friends who abandon you in times of need. They made me feel secure. They made me smile, they told me good things about myself which I have never heard of and momentarily my heart and my mind were calm. Unexpectedly my friends left me, just for those few hours. I started longing for that few hours of freedom, that few hours of peace from their persecution. I started figuring out ways to make those hours longer. I started learning things to do which they detest so they would leave me alone. I found out both cower before my family, they wouldn't wander about in their presence. So, I started spending more time with them. They hated when I read books or listened to podcasts on how to win over them. They despised me talking about my pain to trustworthy friends. They were revolted by meditation, writing, and embracing any form of art. I could slowly start sensing their revulsion to goof around me. Whenever they screamed dispirited things about me, I would retaliate back more loudly and switch on my favourite TV show or music in high volume nulling their voice. They would shudder when I concentrated on my work and eventually, when I moved to a new place, started meeting new people, I would see them jeer at me helplessly and wander off. I would hear them often contemplating to leave or stay and finally leaving in despair aiding my confidence to beam back.

I was and am in love with my newly found voice, strength, and ways to repel them. I didn't have this strength in me in the past, maybe because some part of me was ok with my life as it was. Now I do have that strength to fight back and want to. Life taught me valuable lessons in a brutal way, and I want to learn from them. Of course, even now my beloved friends visit me occasionally but back in their minds they too know that they must leave me for good, very soon. And I am waiting in anticipation for that day to bid a final adieu to my dear friends, ANXIETY and DEPRESSION.

WRITE A LETTER TO YOUR 5 YR. OLD SELF.

Dear 5 yr. old me,

Yours Truly,

6

THIRSTY TEAR

By Anurag Kumar

◆ ◇ ◆

(This story is based on true life and the names of places and characters have been changed to maintain confidentiality.)

'I sit in a corner - frozen and depressed; my thoughts as frozen as my body. My shivers are hesitant to surface and the tear in my eye quivering to roll. My body is sore with bruises that look like the only ornaments I own. I wish the lines on our palms defined our destinies so that I could blame it for all the injustices towards me. The air around me is always heavy with despair as if the grief on earth has been condensed.'

A harrowing experience like this might be easy to analyze and write about in an objective manner but to live through those is somewhat different. In many ways, it's the social set up of our society that gives encouragement to all kinds of violence on women, and my story is nothing different.

From being in an abusive relationship to bearing the burden of raising my children single-handedly, these millions of moments I have created are wrapped up securely in a single frame. All of these single thoughts get shackled by my memories and they make me paralyzed with confused emotions. But isn't this what we call a living – being haunted by memories whether good or bad?

Will you let me take you on a trip down the memory lane?

I am Mala, the fourth sibling of my 6 sisters and 1 brother. If you are amazed by our family progeny, let me tell you it's 1970's and nothing's unusual for us. When my mother died while I was very young, my father Nagesh worked hard in a government office to provide us with basic needs. Life was tough but we were content.

DISCLAIMER 1- THE WRONG MATCH

If marriage is supposed to be a fairy tale saga, it's all a broken truth. I'm not proud to say that once upon a time I was trapped in this devil's snare myself. The suffocation engulfed me so much that I lost all self-worth. I was 'married' to a man named Vikash who came from an elite family in Munger, Bihar. Before I could even process anything, I found myself decked up in bangles, ornaments, and a red dupatta over my head, sitting in the mandap with 'the man'.

Thus, a timid girl in her intermediate who was very timid and insecure around people, got lost in the world of adjustments and nuances of a perfectly celebrated marriage. Just like any other Indian girl, I too was brought up with the values of wifely behaviour and I went on causing no noise. Little did I know that at every small adjustment I made, the expectation would increase ten folds and I'd be taken for granted. My husband turned out to be Casanova who had no care in the world except for leisure and women. The person I was married to had always dreamt of a fair and pretty wife, an eye candy for him but I was dark and unattractive. That's why he refused to even acknowledge me. The blows of his violent behaviour came every other day and I submitted giving myself all the pathetic reasons I could.

I always smirk at the thought of how the human mind is such a trickster. It doesn't take time for it to turn unwanted behaviour into a habit because that's how it became. While I suffered in silence, the injustice towards me grew.

Life went on but did I tell you there is always a 'but'? Just after a few days of marriage, I got to know that my husband had mental issues. He used to suffer from mental seizures often and this was all hidden from my family. But what choice did I have now? I was tied down by the society and my father refused to provide me with shelter. Once you are married, you are a *'Parayadhan'*. I was falling apart, and I was not trying to save myself. I wanted to watch myself die, crumble, and vanish. The beatings grew and with it, a part of my soul was torn away.

DISCLAIMER 2: RISING LIKE A PHOENIX

I looked at myself as a weak soul with no way out of the devastating hell I lived in. Depression engulfed me and I tried to kill myself by consuming multiple sleeping pills. After all, would you consider yourself dead if you are carrying mini corpses inside you? I was mentally broken while my children – a son, two daughters and one in my womb - were a witness to all.

A few days after the incident, I met a woman named Sushma who counselled me to stand up and speak for myself. "Mala, you don't have to live your life in tears. Take some bold step for your children," she said. It took me to the highest mountain of euphoria, and I completed my graduation. Since my husband was a drop-out, he never allowed me to read and write because he feared I would leave him and his family if I got educated. But nothing was going to stop me now. You know how people gossip when they see someone rising above their standards. "Look, Mala is talking to a strange man," or "Vikash needs to stop his wife from going out," daily fell on my ears but I was having none of it.

After my graduation, I started teaching in the village school to earn some money.

DISCLAIMER 3: WHEN BAD LUCK KNOCKS AT YOUR DOOR

As if my prayers were being answered to break out of this monotonous life, an unfortunate twist came in my life. It was 1981 and we had just gone to bed after getting done with our daily chores. Suddenly, we heard someone banging on our door shouting for my father-in-law. "Uncle, please open the door. My child is sick." Now my father-in-law, Dharam Das who worked as a head clerk in the Forest Department also had extensive knowledge about homoeopathy. People in our village usually flocked to him whenever anyone in their family got sick.

As the banging grew urgent, he opened the door only to be attacked by some robbers. They hit my husband with weapons on his head and injured my father-in-law's right foot. When my mother-in-law refused to give them the key to our safe, the dacoits slashed her with a knife. As blood flowed around our house, they looted all we had – jewellery, money, clothes, utensils. I wanted to protect my children, so we locked ourselves in a room quivering in fear and anticipation about what was happening to my family just a few inches away. I could hear screams of pain and of robbers taking away everything we had. Oh, the nightmare!

Nothing was the same after that rueful night. Once things are killed inside you, no matter how many balms you apply, it's going to stay that way. Ugly scars never heal.

My husband's health continued to deteriorate each day and with it, the abuse towards me grew. What did I say before? You get accustomed to it and you accept it as your destiny, so you keep mum. Was that right? I really don't know. I went to Ranchi to get my husband treated at KK Sinha's clinic and was told that he wouldn't be able to use his brain anymore. The doctor advised me to get him admitted to a mental asylum!

Happiness was a long-lost memory. I had forgotten how to laugh, cry or even talk to anyone. I had resorted to darkness. I was a living corpse. It felt like the lilies were slowly rotting under the mud hole I had dug so happily. When my father-in-law got sick owing to old age, all the responsibilities of the house fell on my shoulders and I did so without a word. In between all that, I also finished my Bachelor of Legislative Law.

One day as we were going on and about our day, my brother-in-law Sunil visited us. He had come with an intention of course and didn't lose much time in demanding my father-in-law to sell his land to arrange money for his daughter's marriage. The poor old man, who had so lovingly taken care of the land and kept it as mortgage to get his sister's married, had no option but to comply. He had worked day and night at a local petrol pump to free the land and here it was, about to slip away from his hand.

My wonderful father-in-law took to the heavenly abode in 1994.

DISCLAIMER 4: THE CITY LIFE

Leaving all the grief behind, I took up a job as a teacher at a private school in Giridih, Jharkhand. We all left for the city with hope for a better tomorrow and went on with our lives there. Soon, I left my teaching job and started practising as an advocate at the Giridih court but not knowing the English language turned out to be a challenge. My husband also took up a job as a deed writer and we both tried to make ends meet. My elder son Ankit also started teaching in a nearby private school to earn money for his further studies and my elder daughter Madhu worked at an organisation named SPEED, a government program to educate people on daily wages.

My miseries and loneliness never ended though and I became exhausted – emotionally, mentally, and physically. The pressure of getting my daughters married in a respected family was weighing me down. I wanted to give my sons a good education, but money was scarce. Who said life was a bed of roses?

Poverty was always a part of our life, but it had never pinched us as it was doing now. I don't even remember the last time I bought new clothes or enough sweets for the guests. We had to manage in just half a litre milk every day of which I had to divide between my youngest child and my mother-in-law.

Gradually, my children grew, and Ankit left home to start his career in Delhi. He took up tuitions to survive in the big city and boy, was I proud of him! With all the snide remarks of my daughter not getting married, she ignored all that and completed her masters and worked at a private shop.

One day, my brother-in-law Sunil visited us again, this time to ask for money for his younger daughter's marriage. Since we were seeing him after such a long time, my mother-in-law's happiness knew no bounds. She wanted to prepare a fancy dinner for him but was turned down. When she showed excitement to attend the marriage ceremony, she was told she wasn't invited. My heart went out to her for such a poorly treatment, but I knew what being a mother meant - you give everything to your child without expecting anything in return.

I somehow arranged money for the wedding because this time I couldn't let him sell our land like before. I also took my mother-in-law to the marriage ceremony.

She died soon after that and Sunil even refused to stay till the end of the cremation ceremony. It's strange how people easily forget the ones who raised them and loved them more than their own life.

DISCLAIMER 5: GETTING MY CHILDREN SETTLED

In the market of dowry, getting the right match for your daughter takes a huge toll. What's love and what's compassion in a marriage? It's all about money and I too struggled with it. In a male-dominated society like ours, I set out to find a groom within 'the right budget' for Madhu. Having a mentally ill husband didn't help much and drove most of the families away. While some had unreasonable demands, some criticized my daughter's looks.

After much struggles, I fixed her marriage with a man from Gaya, Bihar and the ceremony took place happily. At that time, Madhu was working at the block office in a contractual position and had taken a loan for her marriage which she repaid soon.

My youngest son Raushan also took to Delhi to stay with Ankit who was now working in a multinational company. And very soon, my other daughter got married as well.

Now that my children are settled, I often introspect retrospect on what will happen to me and my husband in our old age. Who will look after us? When will we get a house of our own? Will I ever have a garden of my own? I long to die in my own house rather than a rental one and I keep asking people for good deals.

DISCLAIMER 6: A HAPPY ENDING

A single ray of light is enough to help; all you need to do is give fear no space in your soul. You are stronger than you know. With free time in my hand now, I joined a couple of NGOs for women empowerment and child welfare. Through that, I managed to help many women sustain in a better way by proper guidance and support. I voiced myself out loud. Yes, I'm absolutely human and I come with my share of shortcomings. Today I stand independent and strong, setting an example for others to be a woman of their own choices. This is because I believe in the saying 'you are what you choose.' I carry no guilt within for what I am today.

I knew I had taken a difficult path, but I also knew that it wasn't an impossible one. The key to it was that I never stopped learning and I never underestimated myself. I fought all odds, every sickness, poverty, and abuse and rose fiercely.

My mornings now start with talking to my children and listening to their daily rant. That makes my day. Just knowing that they are happy, satisfied and content in their lives makes me go on. My husband still has some bad days where his mental condition deteriorates, and he starts insulting me. I have never once been praised by him for everything I have done for my family, but I have learnt to live with it. That's what encouraged me to stand up for other women and teach them to be independent and confident.

But now, we have grown old and used to each other. He often prepares tea for us both every morning and we sit on the porch talking about tits and tats of life – just random stuff. We both love gossiping and can't stay without it. After all, who can break this powerful bond of marriage? Love is all that matters.

LIKE I SAID IT IS JUST A PAGE, GIVE YOURSELF

AN AUTOGRAPH LIKE A STAR.

7

EVERYTHING CHANGES WITH A SINGLE CONVERSATION

By Amol Gawade

Sometimes, a little push is needed to get the ball rolling. Everyone has a different life and therefore a different battle to fight every day. We have no idea what is happening behind closed doors or even worse, inside closed minds. Our minds can be a scary place at times. When they don't allow us to function in our day to day routine, we start to see the cracks in the perfect exterior.

Despite the fear of being perceived as intrusive, it's important to remember that when it comes to mental health, checking in with someone reminds them that they aren't alone when they've gone quiet.

They can come from those closest to us, like our parents, or friends and colleagues who have never experienced mental illness. They try to be sympathetic but the words they choose to use can sometimes feel like a knife in the back.

There are definitive moments and decisions in my life that have led up to my depression. In the summer of 2012, at the age of 19, I found myself struggling with depression more than ever before. Low motivation, low moods, no energy to do things. You can't tell just by looking at someone whether or not they have depression. And it was for that very reason that mine went unnoticed by people around me. With the massive stigma surrounding depression, I never told anyone. Study & daily routine work became increasingly difficult to show up to; I feared to confide in anyone about my mental health because I saw myself as a burden.

I felt like I'd be draining to listen to, not worthy of being cared about. With my self-esteem at rock bottom, I couldn't even begin to appreciate the empathy of others. Depression had completely changed my life.

Some people think that depression is just a bad day. But actually, it is a long-term mental illness. Depression is more than just sadness. It's having no feelings at all. It's overthinking or not being able to think at all. Those emotions are not always acknowledged by those around you. Instead of helping, some people tell you to "get over it". Mental illness is not something you can simply "get over".

When I had issues with motivation, it was made to look like laziness. Low moods hidden by fake smiles.

All my friends were enjoying the long bright days, maximizing the warm weekends, going on adventures, getting engaged, and house hunting whilst I became increasingly isolated, on the outside looking in.

Days passed wishing someone could see me and my pain. I wanted to talk about how much I was struggling but didn't know-how. I feared to scare others; it became excruciatingly a routine to just ignore the phone. Depression became my world; I couldn't imagine anyone else wanting to see inside so I pushed everyone away. I didn't want to drag them into my own turmoil.

I'd experienced periods of low mood but depression in its entirety overwhelmed me, I felt trapped in my loneliness, convinced that no one wanted to hear the truth about how I was really feeling when they asked.

There are unwritten rules for answering certain questions. When people ask: "How are you?" they expect to get the statutory "I'm fine thanks, how are you?" Not: "I feel like I'm falling apart, and I can't cope," or "I don't know how I'll get through the day," or some other variation of the hellish truth. That makes for a rubbish situation where, even when you get texts or actual face-to-face inquiries into your wellbeing, you skirt around it or make something up or dismiss it.

It was easier to shut people out in and outside of the home with the classic "I'm fine" when in truth I was falling apart, bereft with the fatigue of life becoming progressively joyless.

Inside I knew that if a friend was having a tough time, I'd want to know how they were really doing just so they knew they had a friend on the other side of the walls around them. I'd never been in the habit of giving up on people but struggled not to give up on myself.

I'd spent my life giving my time, energy, love, and patience to others yet couldn't imagine getting back in return. I didn't know how to accept help because I couldn't believe I was worthy of it.

Weeks of avoiding social contact had passed, and a close friend reached out for me. He wanted to see me, catch up and see how I was, we had formed a really close bond from childhood days and though my walls were still up I let him in. He thankfully wasn't buying it when I said I was "fine". The fact that he was persistent with communication despite me being consistently unresponsive pushed me to realize that hearing from him really added to my willingness to at least try and open up. It reminded me that I had a real friend out there, that I was cared about.

Despite the walls depression encouraged me to put up, I'd learned it's okay to take a few bricks down and talk to the person on the other side.

We sat over dinner talking about work, summer plans, and books we'd shared an interest in. I mentioned not having read much recently because I couldn't bring myself to do it. Then came the dreaded question.

"So, how are you?"

I sat there speechless, eventually telling him I couldn't answer that.

It felt like a loaded question.

As a society, we've become accustomed to seeing conversations about negative thoughts and feelings as something to be ashamed of yet talking about having the flu is seen as normal.

"Seriously, just say whatever comes to mind. I want to know how you're feeling."

That push right there, he is asking me for a second time led to me opening up about feeling low, desperately unhappy, and not enjoying life.

It steered to me to explain why I struggled to keep up with reading, about leaving things and what I'd like to move on to. I didn't feel like I had to filter what I was saying so it all just came out; the dam of pent up emotion had burst its banks.

He never judged me, only listened.

We didn't spend the whole evening talking about my mental health, we just talked. My mental health disorders haven't vanished and still cause me no end of pain, but I can finally see a light at the end of a very dark tunnel.

The times I have felt most supported have been over a cup of tea, talking freely about my conditions, without fear of judgment. I still have days when I am looked at in pity or told to 'Smile, it's not the end of the world'.

The fact is that people with mental illness are not often talked about badly anymore, it seems we are just, quite simply, not talked about, not in any meaningful way anyway. I saw people sending posts on my Facebook and WhatsApp with one-off little comments on how they've struggled, and that's great. That they share their condition with me, and it gives more power to them. There is no substance to them. It actually works for me to uplift my inner strength and think positively towards things of life.

Those with mental illness don't need a quick fix. We don't need lots of presents. We don't need to feel guilty that we didn't speak out sooner. We don't need to be reminded of how lucky we are and how it could be worse. It requires listening, to check-in, to educate yourself, to accept this part of life. To understand that what we are going through is real and the longer it is hidden away, the longer it takes for us to bring it into the open and get support.

There is always one person for everyone to whom you can open up & tell that person whatever you think. That openness & motivation from self - belief to deal with my mental health. It opened my eyes to really think about all the times I've said I was fine when I wasn't, and when others around me have done the same.

People are more than happy to talk about their "success" in recovery, but very few will talk about the constant risk of relapse, or their bad days. This gives the wrong message that mental illness is something to be "overcome", rather than live with. There is a lot out there in the world, a lot of noise, but I wonder if we cut through the politics and the media hype, we may find that just talking might help.

To anyone reading this, A friend with a mental health problem is still a friend, a life with mental health problems is still a life. Always remind yourself that they aren't invisible and that they will be heard. Remember it is ok to speak out. Please do not suffer in silence. Silence is painful, soul-destroying and will never help you. You do not become anything less to your true friends when you tell them you're not doing so well. You will always have someone thinking of you because those with mental illness are never alone. If there are 7 people in a room with you, chances are one of them is struggling too.

The more people that share their experiences the fewer people will feel isolated. Talking about mental health and building understanding could definitely save many lives.

So, never let your circumstances define who you are; you can be anything!

Break the Silence. Break the Stigma.

DRAW SOME MORE EARBUDS.

8

HIDDEN DEEP WITHIN

By Arati Harikumar

—— ◆ ◇ ◆ ——

She sat by herself in one of the most crowded cities in the world and never ever in her life had she felt so lonely. She loved living in Mumbai only because she could seek solace in the Arabian sea. The sea always had a calming effect on her, watching the waves while the sun waved her goodbye and the sound of the waves enriching her soul; in those instants' serenity would take over her mind. The waves crashed back and forth, ushering in memories – some that she dreaded to forget but most that she dreaded to retain in her memory closet. That is the thing with memories, they reach out to you when you least expect. And then they play with your emotions just like her favourite game of catch-and-cook she remembered playing as a kid. She hates it when this happens. Wiping the sweat from her forehead, she stared into the setting sun. Her gaze was so fixed and powerful, even the hawkers avoided pestering her with their wares. She only saw the sun and heard the waves and everything else ceased to exist. The turmoil in her heart never showed on her face. Just like the waves crashing on the rocks, the reminiscences touched her soul engulfing her in grief she had never known.

To describe Prerna in one word would be exceedingly difficult; she was so much more than what one person could ever describe her. An independent, happy-go-lucky, smart woman who was well-loved and admired by her friends, family, and colleagues, she carried herself with quiet dignity, ease and had a calming aura – one you could easily sense when around her. This coupled with a curious mind and childlike enthusiasm quickly made her a favourite in her circles. The first time she met Shreyas, she felt nothing extraordinary about him. It was a usual formal meeting at her work which he was a part of. They stayed in touch professionally and over a period of time became friends. To say he was charming and good looking would be an understatement. While he was that, he was also a good orator with excellent convincing skills, extremely confident and could easily captivate anyone with his stories. He could regal an audience with ease. Prerna had never met someone quite like him. As time passed, the friendship blossomed which gradually turned into love; their chemistry was electrifying. Defying all odds, she changed cities to be close to him. And just as how it goes, everything was smooth in the beginning. The fact that Shreyas loved living life at an edge never bothered her much. He was always so supremely confident, and she knew there was nothing to worry about.

Today as she sat staring into nothingness, she shivered at how Shreyas would drive. It was easily one of most times she spent with him; long drives because they both loved it. He would be drinking for hours and by all means, he would be very stubborn about driving. No amount of reasoning worked. He would drive like a maniac cutting across lanes, by lanes and zipping past every other vehicle. If the speed limit was 80, he would be at 180 easily. That would happen often and would end up with him requiring validation from Prerna on how he is the best in everything, how he defines odds, he is the one who creates the rules. He makes them, he breaks them. She often asked herself if his constant need to be the best, to be validated was normal but then rationalized that some men who claim to be alpha males and with a personality such as Shreyas's would not be easy to handle but definitely, there was nothing to worry about. Never, was she so wrong.

A little pup interrupted her thoughts, as it chased a ball and leaped on to her lap in excitement. She smiled and cuddled it before the frantic owners, a middle-aged man and woman came to take claim of him. Smiling to herself, she remembered Maggie, the golden Labrador who kept her sane when she was living or rather hiding from Shreyas and his frenzied behaviour. Strangely this memory made her cringe and she was amazed at her own reaction.

There was never one day where things went wrong or maybe there was, but she never saw it. There were too many wrongs till the path of right and wrong camouflaged within one other creating ripples of confusion in her mind. Ripples that he created so successfully over a period of time. At times, she wonders how she could have been trapped in something so devastating to a human mind.

Prerna knew something was wrong, very wrong with Shreyas within the first 3 months of living in Hyderabad. To begin with, he didn't have a job as he claimed he did, he didn't even have any consulting contracts (again what he had told her). When she realized that he was relying on her for running a home including his expenses, she began to worry. Her questions were met with evasive responses. And because he had convinced her that he was her knight in shining armour, she believed him. Blindly. Maybe even deafly – nothing else could enter her brains, it was as if she was hypnotized. Slowly she began to sense that he was living on her hard-earned money, he had no job and nothing to look forward to. The picture he painted of being a popular man with a high demanding job was a façade. He clawed on her with every opportunity he got; nothing she did was good enough. One evening, after fighting some resistance from Shreyas, Prerna went to meet some friends. By the time she was home, he created a ruckus pointing fingers at her character. The yelling and screaming brought the owner of the building to check if she was ok. He behaved like a frenzied human, throwing her things from her cupboard, asking her to leave him all the while yelling and screaming. The next morning when she stood her ground and told him off, he had changed into an angel. He caressed her and begged her to forgive him. He was even touching her feet begging for mercy. These instances with Shreyas became a pattern. Over the months, each of these repeated. Each worse than the other. At one time the yelling and screaming were so terrible that he broke things in the house and almost came to hit her. It was then it dawned on Prerna on how abusive this man could get. To make matters worse, she was blamed for arousing his anger and ensuring he would hit her - it was what she said, what she did, how she spoke and even how she walked. She was always the one to blame.

As hard as she tried, she could not make him see sense. He would use her arguments against her, it felt like he was living in her mind-reading her thoughts and outsmarting her in every way he could. Her confusion and pain only increased, she didn't know what this was and what was she to believe. While he was wooing her, he would often speak of women empowerment with passion; however, she found him making contradictory remarks often in conversations and degrading remarks especially in front of colleagues. It was as if he hated women. With a shocking understanding, she realized she was dealing with a misogynistic individual. Prerna didn't know who Shreyas was anymore. Nothing he ever told her and promised her made any sense. She was living with a man who was a control-freak, who was abusive, who was two-faced and to make it worse, he read her like an open book challenging her to save herself. All her attempts to make him understand her view was met with sarcasm and condescending remarks. She was at a complete loss. The man she thought she met and who she loved was not him, it was as if she was dealing with a stranger, every single day. She was confused and her mind ranged with unspoken thoughts and doubts.

The answers to those questions surprisingly came from Shreyas himself. She was visiting her parents over a weekend and got a frantic call from him. He was drunk and yelling at her. The reason for this scene leaves her amused even today as she picks up some stones from the pavement for no reason. He was angry at her irresponsible nature of not drawing a 'Kollam' outside the house. Kollam is a south Indian tradition followed by few communities to attract positive energy. She was stumped and tried reasoning with him – everything from the fact that she doesn't see a reason to do this, she is unaware of how this is done and the biggest reason – she is not in Hyderabad at the moment. But the yelling and screaming persisted for more than an hour till she told him she is never returning to him. Almost instantly, he was transformed into a puppy begging her not to leave him and promising her the world at her feet. Exasperated and tired with his mind-games, just when she was about to disconnect the line, he begged her and screeched into the phone about his neglected childhood and how it should be easy for her to handle him, only if she learns how to handle a narcissist. She could not believe what she heard. She threw one of the stones at the sea, it didn't even land anywhere close to where she wanted but the revelation of this memory made her smirk at herself. How did the universe even conspire this message to reach her and that too from him?

Prerna's instinct was to help Shreyas. Always the giver, she tried to coax him to see psychiatrists or psychologists which never happened. Every day from there on was a living nightmare. His verbal abuses were at their peak coupled with extreme mood swings. Nothing she ever did was right. His abuses ranged from her cooking skills to comparing her with his ex-girlfriends and destroying her every single day. He had no regard for her feelings and did everything to bully her. He would stonewall all her attempts to reach out to him. Looking back, she knew that his every move was well-thought of. He introduced her to his family and later would use that to emotionally blackmail her to be with him or to ignore his flaws. This went on for almost a year. It was a pattern with him. Every single day she felt she was losing a part of herself and she didn't know what she could do. She never mentioned the challenges to anyone; she was too afraid to be judged. The answer to her situation came in the form of her mother who rescued her.

Her relationship with Shreyas reached its boiling point one evening when she questioned him about the money, he owed her. Shreyas threw a fit yelling at her and drove off in his car. He kept calling and yelling at her, abusing her and her family. That was the final straw. When it was unbearable, she left. Just like that, with whatever she could gather. Her mother was her saviour and a driving force who held her hand and stood by her. However, Shreyas had complete control over her finances and also on her to a large extent. It was as if he read her like an open book – what would she do, how she would react, how she would think, who would she speak with, chat with – he knew her like the back of his hand. He knew her psyche. The battle was far from over.

Prerna took shelter with a kind family who let her stay with them. Her best friend knew of this family and arranged for the stay. Prerna closed her eyes and thanked them for their generosity, this was a debt she would never be able to repay in this lifetime. To be taken care of by people who know nothing about you defines kindness and love at an unexplainable level. But Shreyas didn't give up. He threatened to kill her, to destroy her. He knew her email passwords and changed them denying her access to her emails, he would track her on google maps, sending her repeated messages which only scared her further. His calls were frantic and crazy he would repeatedly call and message her incessantly at odd hours. This was never-ending. He would threaten then cry and beg her to not leave him. He even went as far as to message her parents and use abusive, degrading language with them. He created WhatsApp groups of her family and friends and spread stories about her, none of them true. Everything with him was an exaggeration. As if all this wasn't enough, he went as far as to email her best friend at her work ID and share her private pictures with her. He would not stop at anything to destroy her. Prerna closed her eyes at the memory, she couldn't believe what she went through. She was so scared and petrified of him, she took another SIM and went to live with her uncle in Mysore for a few days. However, she had to return to Hyderabad sooner or later. There was no easy way to escape him.

When Shreyas figured where she was staying, he reached at 4 am near the house to meet her badgering her with calls and messages for hours. The family she stayed with, held her at good stead explaining the practical way out and why she should not give in to these demands. Logically he had no demand, he just wanted her to be with him. And there was no way she was ever going back to a manipulative, psychotic man. After changing her number, she moved to a hostel so that he would not trace her. That was where she met Maggie, the golden Labrador who was her companion for weeks. No one except her family and best friend knew where she was. She was off all social media and maintained no contact with anyone. Even today, she recollects the place so vividly, though it seems like a lifetime ago. The dormitory, the rooms, the people, the food – it was as if she was another person living in another era. Prerna would skip meals for days to avoid expenses. Most days she never knew what hunger was. The hostel dormitory was her sanctuary, she felt like every step away from there would mean Shreyas trying to kill her or harm her. His threats with emails continued and she would spend lonely nights staring at the rotating blades of the fan above her. She hardly had the energy to leave her bed or eat or sleep or even think. At nights, she would watch the silhouettes of other women in the dormitory and their movements. Sleep eluded her. Every time there was a vehicle passing by and when the brakes screeched, she would tremble inside her blankets and pray that he doesn't find her. He never did but try as hard as she could, those memories never left her.

Shreyas's threats didn't change and this time he wrote to her a suicide email along with messages to her parents threatening them. By then Prerna had had enough. With what little courage she could muster and with the guidance from some total strangers and her best friend, she finally had the courage to register a police complaint of harassment. With that, Shreyas backed off – just a little but he did. The months of emotional torture left Prerna dead from within; she felt like a lifeless soul. She was so afraid of everything around her – the nights were dark, long and lonely, she was battling demons she never even knew existed. Everything from loud noises to screeching cars to strangers looking at her petrified her. She often wished she was invisible or that the ground beneath her would open and soak her in. Within weeks she was in 3 different cities so that Shreyas could never touch her – body or soul.

She returned home on a humid day; the blazing sun did nothing to ease her worry. She felt no emotion in her, it was as if a part of her died within her. For days together, she would never leave the corner of her bed; she was afraid of darkness, of loud noises, of flowing water or maybe even another human. She never contacted her friends; she just lay on her bed, feeling like the sea that she was watching had swallowed her. She closed her eyes at the memory, tiny sweats escaped her forehead. How did she even come this far? She remembers her home vividly – there were 14 carton boxes plus suitcases to unpack, her home- the place she grew up in was a mess, but she had no sense of time. She only remembers reading – she read every article that was available on NPD or Narcissistic Personality Disorder – how they target their victims, how they brainwash them, how they are so hollow that don't ever feel another human, how they always have a feeling on entitlement, how they are expert liars, how they use gaslighting and stonewalling as techniques to rob a person of their identity. It was all too much to take in at one go but her brain devoured it and her heart was on a roller coaster ride. She realized with a heavy heart that she escaped was not just emotional and verbal abuse, it was something so incredulously damaging that it could have ripped her from herself. It shook the ground beneath her feet. The information was too much, but she took it all in. No one who would have seen NPD survivor at close quarters, no matter how closely will ever understand the trauma they go through. Mainly because they would never know the other side of the manipulator. The mind games that the victim is subjected to is beyond comprehension for most human minds. It is by far the most unexplainable, unimaginable situation one endures. Prerna read about NPD support groups and reading about the stories of others gave her some courage and fortitude to move on. She smiled meekly at herself, such a journey this has been. Little by little, she tried to put her life back on track. Every day she woke up with renewed faith; with the help of her family and close friends she learned to live. It was as if a child was learning to walk – each step was scary and yet vital.

The waves once again broke her reverie. And while the sunset and dusk prevailed in front of her enveloping the city of dreams, a single tear escaped her eyes. The dawn had broken, somewhere within her.

WE SEE DREAMS EVEN IN DAYLIGHT BUT FOR NOW, JUST DESCRIBE/DRAW A DREAM THAT YOU SAW AT NIGHT.

9

THE DARK U-TURN

By Shagun Salecha

— ◆ ◇ ◆ —

The glamorous and lucrative shine of life and its spark lures people within itself. The dawn of a day comes with the rush for running down with the struggles of life and trying to achieve the best we possibly can. The race just engulfs each one of us into itself in such a manner that escape seems merely impossible. Life takes a U-turn facing those bitter realities we all are scared to admit and proceed further. Some people have the striving ability to move on with it, while some are stuck.

The usual morning starts with a beautiful sunrise with the sun reminding us of the goals we set ourselves to conquer and with time, the sunset helps us reflect back and think how far we've come. The story is about a young, brave, and budding girl. Each day having the courage to keep moving on forward requires hope and an immense amount of strength. This girl is carrying a pile of books, setting out to live her everyday routine, she initially had someone to hold on to, someone who could comfort her, guide her. She believed in her parents blindly and made them proud of all her little actions. She made her parents happy and sometimes her certain moves made her realize to choose between right and wrong. Life moves simultaneously in different directions, and following this pattern, she was made to learn to be responsible. The diversifications grew more complex, like a dendritic pattern, with the streams moving slow and expanding collectively. The time is highly crucial and difficult, she had the support and confidence of her parents, which made her decide to give it a start. The introduction of something entirely new in her life was scary but she was prepared. She was a budding seed from the ground that did break through the atrocities of small weeds, insects, and the other barriers. It was the time when she was first sent to a boarding school. It seemed very glittery, fancy, exciting and as a huge arena of positivity. This was the time for her to step out of her world, her comfort zone, and seek her potential that people who believed in her knew she could achieve.

It is said every choice you make leads up to what you're going to be in the future. The commencement of the new life was marked with one small incident. This incident was a mere moment, as mere as someone coming right next to her with a bleak informal introduction, but later it became of a greater significance. The life in that small place was a new world altogether. That small incident was marked of utter importance due to the repeated reminder of the feeling that certain small and hidden things are the best and worth it.

The time passed by teaching her a lot of things from standing for herself at bleak times, in unfamiliar and difficult situations to others.

There was a time when she had to say goodbye to her small little world and go home. The parents decided to shift her to a place. The small secure world was a feeling of having a new family.

This journey took her on a pedestal, where she felt insecure about having roots from a safe and secure environment to a platform where she could be vulnerable to mislead herself from drawing a thin line between right or wrong. The ability to choose between the shades of grey. It was initially a muzzling experience, where she did fall many times, but a strong will gave her the strength to rise above all the atrocities in life. The day in the school starts and she is thought to be naïve but walks past amongst all those people who are mean, rude and very selfish. The courage she had of not giving up in life and rising up had made her mould in those conditions. There were instances with her in which she was bullied by either publicly being the subject of mockery or commenting on her looks. The time gradually passed by and she learned the art of ignorance and being very firm on not accepting the perception that people impose on her. This courage made her strong and others weak and they could never underestimate her anymore. There was a small incident, where one of the bullies turns up and asks her for help. This was the moment where she proved to herself by not being too selfish to not help but rather by providing a helping hand. The source of her strength was her parents and she did give up quite a few times. The people who turned around and bullied understood the pain and gave her some strength. It was initially very confusing for her, but later she gained their trust. They became one happy family. It felt to her as if the history were repeating itself in her life. There is a saying "Whatever happens, happens for a reason." Coming of many new people and some staying in her life forever marked those five years of her life. The moments where they shared snacks all night or cooking for others or eating her favourite chocolate cakes, they'd be edged in her memories forever. From the late-night talks with her roommates to all the outings. The most cherished moments of her life were the times spent on the stands to eating veg into the non-veg mess. The little experiences of taking stands in a class of doing wrong things together. The rushing of collecting stocking and garters. The late-night mess studies were not only shared notes but also explained in groups and she was given the title of a social worker. The screaming voices heard by the seniors for lines up. The seniors were the most integral part of her life. Respecting seniors was the one thing she always had in her life. The ability to stand up and get motivated and collecting all emergency items like stationery, to other daily objects were sourced through them. These moments passed by, she attended her boards and she completed her school. She made some bonds that would define her strength during her life at school.

This was the foundational stone laid in her personality. She had a very strong personality with the ability to hide her emotions and help others. She learned to express herself independently and realized the importance of the role of parents in one`s life. This journey has been the part and parcel of every hosteller and she managed to conquer her fears, including every set back in her life. Despite everything, she managed to rise above in her life.

The usual ordinary routine of this girl has been of many other students who have to spend time in hostels. 7 years of life away from her parents, 7 years of staying strong, 7 years of working hard for herself sacrificing so much for the greater good instilled so much in her spirit and made her able to ride all the possible storms of life.

The next step was college. There's more to every story. She loses someone very dear and very close to her heart with the moment shaking her mentally, shredding all the confidence instilled in her, making her lose all her strength she gained through making tough choices in the past. This comes like a shock wave making her numb to her surroundings. It's said that time heals everything. Does it really? Does it heal the fear of staying alone in the dark, wanting someone to hold on to that hand? She has been depressed, dull, silent, and scared. She is scared because she couldn't afford to lose anyone anymore. All who matter, she needed them by her side. She could have lost herself. The struggle, the fear was real. She felt chained, mentally, physically, stuck within the boundaries created by the society, which she accepted because she was afraid. The ability to express her through different mediums was merely impossible. She felt like a dull monotonous circle, where she had to be all alone. The feeling of dejection started budding within her. The regular episodes of sitting in isolation and being still for longer durations were coming under notice to her surroundings. The situation seemed in which a colourful blooming flower started to shred all its petals and left behind with thorns and dried leaves. The glittery and flickering spark of the flower was lost somewhere deep down the dark shadows. She started college with a very low level of enthusiasm again. The problem of depression was highly dominant in a reflection of her poor marks, very less interaction with her friends. She was leading a life, where she imagined her dear one and lived in the mere delusion of, she is being surrounded by her. The slow but the prolonged state of sadness started becoming a worry of concern among her family members. She was facing the issues of severe anxiety, crying in the corners for hours. The family members tried to engage in a healthy conversation for distracting her mind. She was completely showing the signs of retaliation by running away, not replying for hours, closing the doors, and completing shutting herself with regards to this topic. The situation was later understood through her silence.

The realization hit hard about her condition to one of her family members. She was then taken to a consultant and where she was diagnosed with depression. This came as a major setback in her life after all her struggles. She was a college student now; at a place, she always wanted to be. But right now, all she felt was a feeling of draining all the energy in an empty vessel, which belongs to none. She started feeling the sense of loneliness, questioning her self-worth. The feeling was a parasite, weakening her from the inside, killing her. The sessions weren't smooth in the starting, she was scared for being judged in the minds of other people. The counsellor made the situation highly comforting and gave her the push until her saturation point. This gave her the strength to release all the painful thoughts from within and let her self-free. She attended the sessions two times a week. Apart from sessions, she used to engage herself in baking, pottery, and many other things. The motivation from one and other subordinates became her strength. The sessions were later highly comforting and allowed her to make choices of lifting herself above all the suffering pain.

The regular counselling sessions were a major difference, a positive factor in her life, pushing her away from her fears. She felt the sense of being worthy with the support of friends and family. She admitted the feeling is highly saddening, but above all decided to move on in life. Always using the medium of expression by writing and connecting herself with different identical people of having faced similar kinds of sufferance and sensing those stories as an inspiration to rise above and look forward to those bright moments, which she missed in her past.

Some people are born with it, while some acquire this sort of determination by using their experiences and suffering to catapult themselves above whatever tires to hold them down. 9 months later, she is the key to holding everything together. For someone who used to draw inspiration from others just to see a glimmer of hope, just to see a silver lining to propel herself out of the atrocities, now she has become one, an inspiration, climbing the ladder of life more wisely. She was able to accept the fact of holding on to the past is not an option. She considers herself wise enough to channelize all the negative energy and pain into working so hard that the end result provides her with the energy to achieve something better.

The life of this young girl has been a story of a trillion girls across the world. I would like to highlight the need to understand and to be sensitive towards these issues. The potential of each person can reach up to its maximum with support and love. The world comprises of people who are very much like us and the best way to achieve our goals is with happiness. The mere concept of carrying all the burdens of life on one's own shoulders is not a solution and let us all learn from the situations or the atrocities the girl had to fight and battle, where we can inspire and strive to live better. This all sums the brightening of the sun to the dark arena of night. The positivity and complexity of the beauty of being happy within oneself are understood through the ups and downs in one life. Problems acts as a constant hurdle in life which we clear one by one and learn the ability to achieve higher in our lives. This young girl has not only been through all the sufferings but explains herself as a warrior by being able to push herself above all this and mark a new beginning.

WRITE SOME RANDOM NAMES.

ROBERT

ROXY SHA

10

A WISE WISH

By Vanshika Agarwal

◆ ◇ ◆

I think living in the Modern World, makes us want to cling on Hope. Life can be a series of events that drive us away from life if we don't cling onto that hope, looking at the travesties possible in modern times. We have got brilliant opportunities all attached with some risk, but like they say what is life without a little risk, it lets me take those ardent decisions that I wouldn't have dreamt of. In my early 20s, I wasn't particularly fond of children and I never dreamt of having one of my own but as they say, you will eventually like the joys life has to offer and even accept them when they knock at your door. And when I think about not having children, I feel at times that I may have willed it to happen upon my life. However, I've learned to make happiness a habit and started to believe in miracles (not in the Panglossian manner though).

So, I'd given up the thought of ever holding Vidit or any child ever again in my arms, until I met an angel.

Looking at children in the mall made me sick, some parents caught me looking at their child so intently that they just took their baby and all the things they'd shopped and disappeared somewhere I won't be able to look at her baby. Whispers, meant to be hushed in a manner so that no one can hear, but I could hear them, they were about me, about how I was unable to bear a child. Some ladies banged their chests really hard with bangled arms at my misery, "Oh! What magic has this forlorn witch cast on my family! It's a tragedy that you married this foul creature Manan" she'd cry out, the Big Lady so that the whole complex could hear. The Big Lady is a strange woman, I think she is tangled with the past and traditions, that make her scary and even hateful, but she's a lovely old lady, my views about her have changed over the course of time. All she needs is love because that's how love grows.

Some pitied me, some mocked me, some sighed at me, but no one let me be like I was normal. I realized it was a phase and it would come to an end.

There were days when I was excited to go out, have a drink, enjoy a party. I was excited and happy about the how the day would unfold, I would take out my clothes, put aside the accessories that matched and as the evening approached nearer, I would even get decked up, and then it would start. A fear creeping in from nowhere, of not wanting to answer questions of people and not wanting to be looked at etcetera. But in the course of time, I've learned the joy is more about being calm at that moment. Time makes us forget things and teaches us to let go. And if I didn't care, I noticed people wouldn't either. Happiness is to be found in moments we seldom choose for sadness, and that would make you a conqueror.

Because I couldn't bear a child as doctors had declared. I was unfit, it would be a big gamble if I tried to give birth and the odds of winning were sparse. On days, I felt like a coward for not taking risks. So, I tried, and the first time in my fifth month, my water broke and all that happened is still a nightmare. My armour was weak but not my intentions.

It was the first time I met her, at the doctor's clinic and she was sure one of the most beautiful souls God created. "Hello beautiful lady, I am here to make all your dreams come true," she said, smiling widely. We had been waiting for someone to make that promise if it was even possible in adulthood. She would be a surrogate mother for our baby. I cried that day going back home in the car, and as emotions filled me, I wept hard and Manan held me. I knew deep down he was broken too, but he held me. He felt the pain. It felt as if someone had ripped a piece of your heart and mutilated it until nothing remained but a picture of the piece.

So, what was hope? If you ask me it's everything you have left when all from you is taken and life stares at you empty-handed. One has to draw courage to live on and build the hope of putting a life together.

We both were called to the clinic, early that morning, I was nervous. They said it was going to be a small series of tests to see if our embryo would be healthy in Anne's womb. 2 hours passed by. The doctor told us not to worry about anything and that we would be parents of a healthy child in less than 36 weeks. I went inside the room they were conducting tests and hugged Anne tight. Anne was herself a mother of 2 children, her first was ready to go to college next year and her second child, a girl was suffering from polio. Doctors had promised Anne to make her Sarah walk one day. She was to be treated at the Singapore Medical Institute. Anne's husband, Hemant is a good man, the kind of person who we don't meet very often these days. His perspective was well beyond the modern times in a certain way and yet he chose an ordinary traditional life of a Christian household. He visited the church every Sunday, took care of their daughter like an ideal father. He supported Anne in all her decisions. As several weeks passed by, I found a sister in Anne, she comforted me from time to time and as she said, "I inspire her with my fearlessness", which I am not sure is a true statement anymore. Life has moulded me in a certain way these days that the only thing left is self-doubt within me.

36 weeks or less. The doctors were right about the time period, but not about the result. It happened earlier, only in 32 weeks. Mere 32 weeks. It's a lot of time, but it only takes a

second to rip your soul, to believe what's said and the efforts aren't noticed the court of justice, its only karma, what you've been doing knowingly or unknowingly all of it shows up and that's how life is even, that's what I've heard is true.

There are some good days, some bad. Good days are short, you would want them to last forever, but they seem they could be gone in an instant, you want to live every moment, and on bad days, I think this too shall pass. Such was the case when I entered that household that promised me all the happiness in the world. Then why was every moment living in the same drawing-room becoming a mistake? Those confident decisions, I had a feeling grabbed my neck, and pressed hard and willing to let go until I learned to live with the pressure.

And again that moment arrived when we went to the San Delbay Fertility Centre, and that hospital smell of sanitation began to nauseate me, but I walked, it seemed like a long walk but I managed like I'd been doing over the past 17 years, it's a long time to live in insanity and coping with it. I wore a veil and hid under the society described pleasant behaviour. anyway, all tests are done, everything positive. Doctors promised again and I dwelled in the hope which was the only thing that kept me alive.

1 month, we are in a happy place, excitement. Anne comes down every weekend, although we insist, she move with us, but our efforts in vain. She goes to work, where she works as a typist. She's happy with the work. It's easy official work, just the usual. I drop her home at 5 in the evening, which she has

allowed me on my heavy insistence. I go to work, where I am the creative head of a marketing company, owned by a lot of shareholders and chaired by my Father. It's usually interesting work, all the things that are progressive about society. Mostly I find peace there, I busy myself with the work so there is not much left to think about the chores of life.

2nd month, Anne comes down to live with us. She is a cheerful person, sometimes I envy her, it's not the right thing to do. She knows. I know. The fear. It's about attachment. Anne and the baby. Me again with the chores of the world. Scared. But it's her, she, Anne comforts me, she lets me cook for her, we eat on the same dinner table. The big lady of the house is happy with her, so happy, and at ease in a way she never was with me. I am happy about it. Anne's washroom schedule is healthy.

3rd month, things are good. The big lady is in full efforts to keep Anne healthy. I wonder how she has come to love a Christian woman so much that she doesn't feel irritated about her carrying the heir of the house. In the end, Love connects us all in the times we never thought we could comprehend it. Anne visits the washroom every 15 minutes on an average. Anne's husband would visit us often. She went home every weekend.

4th month, I find Manan reading an e-book that's a pregnancy guide, on his laptop. And he's giving tips to Anne, I love his little efforts. I know he tries to man up and support me all the time, but deep inside he too was crushed until Anne walked into our life. The strings of a man's heart and mind are too tangled, but they've learned to veil it with their shield of manhood. Sarah and Anne's husband visited us every alternate day after Miles had left for college. He was a kind soul, studying medicine, staying away from Family to do the best for their futures.

5th month, Anne says she can feel the baby move. She gets occasional kicks and Mr. Doctor has declared the baby healthy. Anne's belly is what I'd call huge and she looks beautiful. Manan has ordered a Fetal Doppler. We are all so very excited and gathered around the couch, Anne in the centre. I put the gel that comes along on her baby bump and move the receiver end over the area. One-minute passes and there's nothing. Another minute. I am scared inside. Then Manan, switches on the Machine (which in excitement, I'd forgotten to switch on) and he asks me to move the receiver once more and there, we can hear a heartbeat, its strong, its beautiful, like a song that connects souls and helps them find enlightenment. I and Manan look at each other locked in a moment. I hug Anne tightly and so does the big lady. Anne squeezes my hand lightly and nods her excitement to me. This moment, I have cherished.

6th month - the bump gets bigger and the pains begin. They are mild. Anne reassures it happened in the past and completely normal.

7th month - the kicking has started in, frequent. I sleep with Anne these days, so as to help her with everything.

8th month-its time, on the 10th of the month of December, our baby couldn't take it further, he displayed signs that he's to be liberated, which caused Anne labour, but it was for the best. Anne shrieked in pain as the pain grew worse, I know it was the pain for joy, the pain that has to be borne to see life evolve. We rushed her to the hospital, it was merely 10 minutes away, but it felt like a lifetime. Manan held Anne's hand; I cleaned her forehead that would fill with beads of sweat. I time to time screamed at my driver to drive faster.

We were in the operation theatre, with Anne at the battlefield, if only fate had given me the chance to be at her place, I would have accepted graciously but my armour isn't strong enough, the Doctors said. I would be weak, a weak person who might end up losing herself in the process if in case, I had the chance. Here Anne was fighting, screaming, pushing, and pushing hard for life, for my life, to save it and to have me experience motherhood. Things in that chamber haunt me certain times but they are for the best and they help me overcome fear. This time I am ready. I held her hand, and kept saying "It's alright, just a little more, just a little further to go ahead". Mr. doctor says within moments of hard work, "I can see the baby's head. Do you want to see it?" I am a strong and confident woman, which is why I fear most things on the inside but let it pass. And as it happens, within moments Anne gives birth to a baby boy, and Mr. Doctor is holding the baby, and tears are trickling down my eyes, as I look at him, so beautiful, he made us wait too long, and almost this time my world didn't shatter inside an operation theatre because I dwelled on hope, not on dreams. Manan held the baby's hand, we both were happy and had tears of joy, that's what they call them. I wished he grew up to be strong like Anne. And I now let Anne hold the baby, she kissed him, and I could say that she was sad, about leaving us and maybe the baby. It was difficult to not be attached, she didn't deny it, she understood, she didn't shed a tear, she was a strong woman. That's why I called her an angel.

IT'S BEEN DARK HERE, HELP ME COLOR THE LIGHT BULBS.

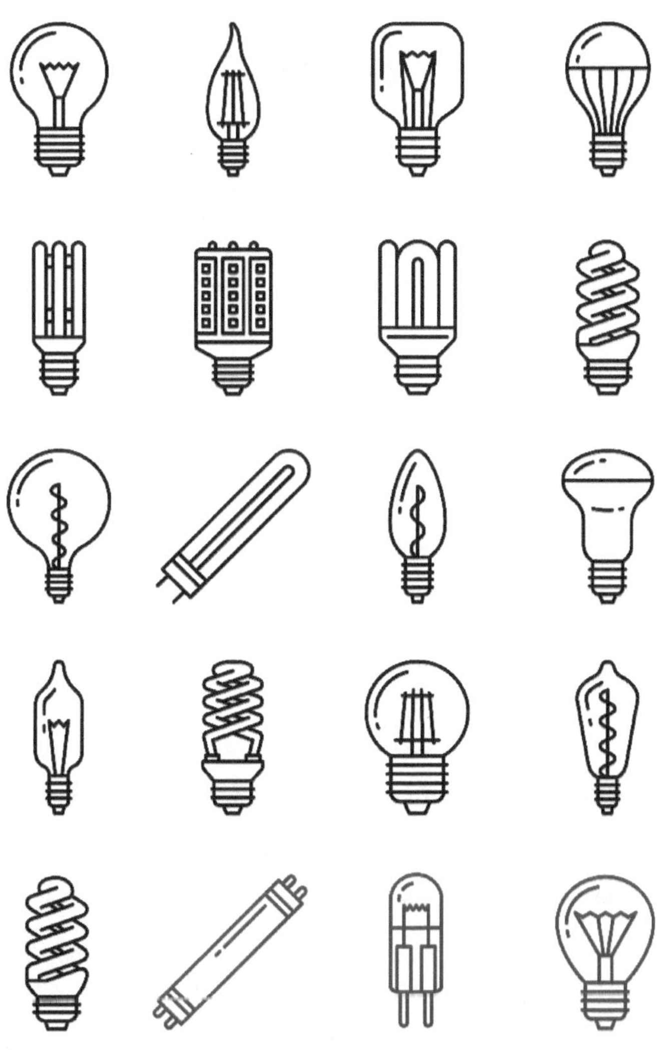

IT'S BEEN DARK HERE, HELP ME COLOR THE LIGHT BULBS.

11

THE CHOICE

By Pritha Samanta

Irritation gives birth to order, and once again, a seemingly worthless winter afternoon is spent cleaning a room. Ira blasted soft music loud on her speakers, as she frantically put things away that day. Her room resonated with the melodies as she lost herself in the moment and focused only on the cleaning. It had been a mess since months, unfolded clothes, laundered and kept in piles, moving from bed to sofa to table and back again, piles of unread books, stacks of unnecessary bills lying around, stationery spread across various places and those irritating pamphlets scattered around the room. It had looked like a rat-feast scene for months. She did not mind the shabbiness; she had learned to work her way around it. But today she had had it. Cleaning for her was never a 5-minute affair. It was an all-in or none kind of commitment. If she wanted a clean table, she needed to put away her makeup, which belonged to her dresser. The dresser currently had books that had to go in her bookshelf. There were lotions lying there, which had to go in her cupboard. There was no space there, so she had to sort her clothes. You see, everything was related.

As she disposed off the last bunch of leaflets, she turned over her phone to look at the time. It was almost 7:00 pm. She had to leave soon if she planned on keeping her promise to her friends. It was a college reunion of 3. She was to meet two of her dearest friends. They had been speaking over calls for so long since graduation. All stayed in different cities now. Chance had brought them together in the same city for a couple of days, and tonight was the night they met.

She quickly stashed off the papers and got up to get ready. She grabbed her trusty white shirt and blue jeans, put her hair in a bun and slipped a long necklace. This had been her go-to outfit for some time. No-fuss, simple and elegant. The necklace somehow gave the illusion that she had put an effort.

Ira walked into the dimly lit café, looking for her friends. They had already arrived and had chosen a table beside the window. 'Perfect', she thought, as she appreciated her decision to put her hair in a bun. She walked up to them, and instantly caught their eye, "Hey guys! How have you been?". "Hey, it's so nice to see you!", "It's been ages since we met!", "How have you been?" they all spoke together and started laughing. "I've been great!" Ira replied, and sat down next to the window. Aisha and Meera looked at her like they were expecting her to say more, but she kept quiet. "So", Meera said, "You have been awfully cryptic about what you are up to these days! Anything new?" "Nothing much!" Ira shrugged, "Just the usual, work and home." "I have had a wonderful year so far, went on a solo trek, and now I am on my way to venture a start-up of my own", Aisha said. "Wow that is so great", Meera said, and Ira smiled proudly.

Aisha had come a long way. She was the typical spoilt single child when she had joined college. All the kids used to make fun of her overtly coddled ways. But time had changed her, and through the four years of grad school, she had seen a transformation like no other. Ira watched as Meera played with her hair, while Aisha told them about how she got her ground-breaking idea on the flight back from a vacation.

Aisha paused for a second in between her story, only to silent a call, and then went on again. "...so as I landed back home, I had to tell my idea to our relationship manager at the bank, you know, to apply for a loan, but luckily, Frank told me about crowdfunding, and....", her phone rang again, "Excuse me, girls, I must take this!", she said, and excused herself.

As she got up and left the table to take her call, Meera looked at Ira. "All okay?" she asked. "Yes, of course. Why do you think otherwise?" she replied. Meera stared at Ira in a 'you know why' kind of way. Ira just stared back. "Well," Meera replied, "You haven't spoken much, all you have done is smile and look out that window." "What do you mean? I have been talking." Ira defended. "No, Aisha has been talking. I have been listening.

You, I am not so sure." Meera replied calmly. Ira just looked down and sipped her water. "Look, I know you have been through a lot." Meera started, "Meera, please…" Ira tried to stop her. "Just listen," Meera pleaded "I know it has been a lot, but I hate to see you like this. Why don't you…" "So, it turns out I have a meeting with a big guy. I don't want to jinx it, so I can't share the deets, but I need to take a rain check. Sorry, Ira, it was so nice to see you again. Meera, you are coming with me, right?" she said it all super-fast while grabbing her shrug from the back of the seat. "Yeah," Meera replied, quickly getting up, startled.

As they hugged out their goodbyes, Meera slipped a card into Ira's hand and whispered "Please just call" into her ear. They bid their farewell and left the place. Ira stared as their cab drove away. She didn't feel like going home in a cab, so she walked. She did not like it when people got nosey and judgemental about her life, but she didn't mind Meera. Meera had been her rock through college, and that woman was always right. She could pick a pearl from a pile of plastic from a distance of fifty feet, and still be right about it. Ira opened the door to her room and sat on her table. She took out the card from her bag and looked at it.

Dr. Jerry Thomas

Therapist / Counselor

'Why does Meera think I should call him? Does she think I am insane? Is this a prank?' She kept questioning herself.

She dropped the card on her table and went to sleep. Today had been weird. 'Let's think about this tomorrow.'

*   *   *

Dr. Jerry Thomas was a tall, thin man. He wore round specs that were perched right at the tip of his long, sharp nose. His plaid 3-piece suit made him look like a bit of an outsider in this sunny weather. He walked animatedly across the room with his angular limbs and plopped himself on the single tan couch. "So, Ms. Ira, you sounded confused on the phone. I almost didn't know whether you wanted an appointment or if it was a prank call. Would you like to say something about that?" Dr. Thomas started.

Ira was fairly surprised herself that she was here. That night, after dinner with Meera, she had kept seeing Meera's face all night. It wasn't a dream. Dreams are much more realistic. They are understandable. This was like a ghost. It was like an image in smoke that had kept following her with every toss and turn. It kept on repeating the same words "Just Call!" Ira's attempt at sleeping that night seemed completely fruitless. She lay half asleep all night, and just like many other horrific pranks of life itself, she fell asleep at 6:00 in the morning, had woken up with a start at 9, and called in sick at work. She had stumbled across the room to her table, found the card and dialled Dr. Thomas' number in a daze.

A bird on the window brought Ira back to the present. "I don't know", Ira mumbled meekly. Dr. Thomas looked at her and said, "Very well! Since I don't know what you want, but you are here anyway, I will start with some basic questions about you. Please answer honestly, I am not here to judge you." he smiled. "What is your full name?" he asked, opening his notepad and positioning a pencil on top of it. "There," Ira thought, "whether I like it or not, I am seeing a shrink now." "Ira Singh", she replied staring at her hands on her lap.

"Age?" he asked.

"25", she replied.

"Job?" he went on.

"Graphic designer", she said.

"Hobbies?" he asked.

Ira looked up startled and stared at Dr. Thomas, half expecting him to start laughing. Who asks a 25-year-old what their hobbies were anyway? Dr. Thomas stared back at Ira. His face clearly looked like it expected a reply.

"I used to sing and read books, but these days I don't have much time." She mumbled.

Dr. Thomas scribbled something onto his notepad and looked up. "Office timings?" he asked.

"Technically it is 9:00 to 5:00, but the 5:00 is quite flexible", she smiled.

"Well, tell me more about your office", Dr. Thomas said.

Ira went on to describe how her office is situated near the beach, and how they had initially hired her as a content writer. She had shown a knack for design, so she had been chosen for a workshop. One thing had led to another, and she had become a designer at the firm.

Dr. Thomas nodded along and scribbled in his notepad as Ira told her story. When she was done, Dr. Thomas looked up and said: "What did you enjoy more?"

Ira stared at him and said, "What do you mean?" "Which job did you like more, that of a content writer or that of a designer?" he asked. "I was promoted to a designer from a content writer. It was an entry-level job; it didn't pay much." Ira blabbered staring at him as though he was being stupid. "I understand Ms. Ira, but as I understand, both jobs need very different skills. They exercise different parts of your brains, require you to see the world differently. Which did you enjoy more?" Dr. Thomas asked patiently. Ira remained silent. "You need not answer me now Ms. Ira. In fact, you need not answer me at all," he said. Ira stayed quiet, thinking of reasons to justify herself. Did she like writing more? Maybe Dr. Thomas was wrong, and she liked designing more. She was not sure. Is it possible that she didn't like either?

"Our time is almost up today, but I would like to ask you something. When you called, you were talking about this friend of yours, who gave you my number. Why do you think she recommended a counsellor for you?" he asked.

Ira looked up from her lap after a couple of minutes, looked straight at Dr. Thomas in the eye and replied, "My boyfriend of 6 years died in a car accident 2 years ago."

*   *   *

Ira didn't think much of her meeting with Dr. Thomas. He had at the end of the session asked her to come again in a week. "It is an open appointment" he had said. It was up to her if she wanted to come or not. Ira did not think she was going. She didn't see how it was helping her be better. If she needed that, that is. She went around in her life, going to work, coming back, eating and sleeping like she always did. Once or twice she asked some of her random colleagues what their hobbies were "What do you mean?" Jessica had said, "Reading, maybe", Ana replied, and Jeremy had just laughed it off.

Thursday was coming in, and she found herself thinking about Dr. Thomas. He had not forced her to do anything she didn't want to. Maybe his questions were leading her somewhere. Meera had suggested his name, maybe she had a reason. So, soon, Ira found herself back at Dr. Thomas' office. They chatted about her college, her life in school, her parents and whatnot. She found herself going back to Dr. Thomas ever week. She never sought any answer. Nor did Dr. Thomas give any. Days went by, and they kept seeing each other every Thursday evening at 7:00 PM.

"Who do you like more? Dad or Mom?" he had asked once and made Ira angry. He wasn't bothered much about her anger. He went on and asked her some other questions. "Why do you trust Meera?" "Does your brother know the real you?" "Who is your best friend?" she sometimes felt like she was answering to a 5-year-old, yet these are the questions that made her think. She had started enjoying her sessions with Dr. Thomas. The initial feelings of vulnerability were almost gone, and now, she had started questioning herself, her life and her decisions.

One day, almost 8 weeks since they had started meeting, she went to Dr. Thomas' office and found the cabin locked. She checked her voice mail for a message or a text, but there were none. This had never happened before. Maybe he had forgotten about their appointment? She didn't think so. Maybe something urgent had come up and he had to leave. She went back home and sat down on her table. This is where it all started, she thought to herself, as she found herself fiddling with Dr. Thomas' card.

She took out her phone and called up Meera. "Hey Meera, how are you", "Great, so nice to hear from you", she replied. "How is life?", "Great actually!" Ira replied, "I took your advice." "What advice?", Meera asked. "I am seeing Dr. Thomas. You gave me his card, remember?" There was silence for a few seconds. "Meera?" "Hey, I am so sorry Ira. I really am. I had no idea when I gave you his number that..." Meera said and paused. "That what Meera? He has been great? What do you mean you are sorry?" Ira asked. "You don't know? It came in the news today. That guy was a fraud. He wasn't a psychologist; he was a writer. He posed as a psychologist as he wasn't earning enough as a writer. He had a lot of patients, and he posed as a therapist to con money out of them. I am sorry Ira; I did not know", Meera said. There was a long pause on the line as Ira contemplated what had just happened. She had been played. Played by a writer. "It's okay Meera, you didn't know," Ira replied and kept the phone.

She did not understand this. Dr. Thomas or no wait, Mr. Thomas had been so nice to her. He had asked such amazing questions. He made her think about herself. He made her question her decisions and put a stop to her go with the flow attitude. That was a good thing, right? Who was this person who she had been believing all this while? Did he even make any sense? Where was he now? She needed to speak to him. She searched for the newspaper and found an article about him on page 3. It said that he was arrested and taken for questioning. He had 2 kids and lived in a small house across the street from his office. In his statement, he had said that he loved writing and listening. He had begun writing because of his love for listening to stories, and it was this love for listening that had made him pass off as a therapist for so long.

Ira was heartbroken to read this. The man that she had trusted had betrayed her. Once again, she had found herself alone. She started sobbing and read the rest of the article. His kids were in high school, and he and his wife were separated. She was truly angry and in pain when she read the last line.

Upon questioning him as to why he chose to be a therapist out of everything else, Mr. Thomas had said "I don't know exactly why, but I had a daughter. She committed suicide a few years ago, and in her note, she had written that she had no friends. I guess I wanted to teach people how to be a good friend."

Oh! Ira finally understood why Mr. Thomas had done what he had done. She had needed a friend too. Meera and Aisha were there, but they were far. Aman had been gone a couple of years, and Ira did not have friends. Was Mr. Thomas her friend? Had she become closer to her colleagues? Were they her friends? Who is a friend anyway? How do you define one? Maybe Mr. Thomas was right. Maybe Ira did prefer writing over designing.

DESCRIBE A FUNNY HAIRCUT OR A HAIRSTYLE THAT YOU SAW.

12

THE JOURNAL OF COUNTLESS

By Simran Saxena

June 11, 2008

We moved back to Mumbai from Pondicherry five days ago. This is not something that I am looking forward to. Some appalling events have occurred. First and foremost, I lost my personal journal that I had been maintaining since grade seven. I still remember the time when I was so new to this world of secret diaries. I saw my elder brother's friend from school, Dheera, in the library jotting down something in her fat hardbound fancy-looking notebook, one usual school day. I had met her a few times earlier, mostly the meetings took place after school when I would go stand next to my brother after having said bye to all my friends, ready to go back home. There was a fixed spot where he and his friends would stand, right next to the school ground entry gate, below a colossal banyan tree. What attracted me to this intriguing process was the concept of decorating the cover of the diary. I still remember my muse had covered her diary with a bright yellow paper and pasted some green sequences on them, resembling a heart shape I surmise, and she wrote in it with an orange pen which had a pink feather attached to its cap. Fascinated by these stationeries I approached her while she wrote in her diary.

"Hi, what are you writing?", I asked. "Hello, Siara! Is it your library period now? Oh this, this is my secret diary", came the reply. "What is a secret diary?", Dheera very patiently explained the entire concept to me, "A secret diary is your own personal diary that you write in each day. Every day after the lunch break and before going to bed I write about how my day was, what all happened in the day." "Oh, you ask why? Well, I do not want to forget anything in my life." she said. "You write everything?", I asked. "Yes, I write the diary as if an unknown person is going to read it. Whatever comes to my mind, I just ink it down. I mention every elaborate detail that I can. In this way, I will be able to cherish every little detail of my life." These are the lines that still, even after two years, play on repeat in my mind every time I sit down with my diary. That, I guess, justifies my elaborate style of writing.

How I got my first diary is a story that I want to cherish forever. All the explicit details about its purchase covered the first few pages of my previous diary. That day when I learnt about a personal journal, while heading back home, I very distinctly recollect sitting by the window in my school van thinking of different ways of decorating my own diary. Back in the day, I was a crazy fan of Powerpuff Girls, a cartoon show that aired on television every evening at five. So, I decided that the cover of my book will be filled with all the Powerpuff Girls stickers that I had collected over time. The brakes of the van screeched, on my left was our place of residence. I got down of the maroon twelve-seater vehicle and ran up three floors as fast as I could, followed by my brother panting. I could not wait to discuss my newfound allure with my mother. I asked her if I could get a secret diary, to which she agreed after a questionnaire round which comprised of questions such as what it is exactly, how I would use it and who told me about it. Now that I think of it, she probably always knew about it and was possibly just helping me feel important, like most times when parents interact with children. We waited for the sun to set, mother did not like the sunlight heat and after drinking milk we set out for our quest to find my diary.

However, our first stop was the dairy shop. I looked at my mother with a confused gaze and she replied, "Just a minute, honey." I remember being very restless, constantly pulling her blue dupatta while she spoke to the shopkeeper. After a minute, that seemed more like an hour, we walked away from that store. Soon we reached our next stop, the bookstore. This was a store that I would visit very often with my mother. They had this barter system where mother would take a new short-length book, she told me they are called novels and scolded me once when I drew shapes and painted the pages of it, I was roughly eight then, in exchange for a novel that she had chosen in the previous visit. Usually, the visits were after a gap of one week, relying completely on the calculating skills that I owned back then. While mother would select her choice of new novels for the week, the store also had a small section displaying notebooks, with colourful and attractive covers, I was always found in this section. The covers ranged from different types of animals, bikes, landscape to even cartoon characters. I very distinctly remember a Minnie-Mouse cover notebook that I purchased from there once. So even during this visit, I ran almost immediately as an involuntary action to that spot of notebooks. All the notebooks were stacked one on top of the other and distributed among four levels of shelves. My hands could only reach the second shelf, so during my selection procedure I may have dropped a few books placed at an unreachable height, but that was the most important decision of my life, it had to be made right. Finally, after dropping a zillion books, I got my dream journal. It was there on the top shelf, a blue coloured Powerpuff Girls diary! Looking at it, I screamed out loud, "Mumma, I want that one!" pointing my index finger at the shelf standing on my toes as high as I could. I still remember how excited I was about my purchase and couldn't wait to show it to my brother and father.

I hear my mother, that is my call for dinner. I have to go now.

June 13, 2008

Oh no! I completely forgot to complete the story day before. Continuing from where I left, I still remember how I spent that night sticking all my stickers around the book and filling in my details on the first page. That night, I ditched my teddy bear and slept with my diary instead. The following morning, I packed my textbooks and also slid in the diary without my mother noticing. It was one of my priced possessions and the twelve-year-old me would definitely want to flaunt it. I vividly remember that day in school. During the lectures, in between breaks I would show my friends a sneak peek of the book from my school bag. At break time, after showing it to all my friends I ran to my brother's class to show it to Dheera. On seeing my book, Dheera was as elated as I was. Getting that thumbs up from her meant the world to me.

The sad part is, while relocating to Mumbai back from Pondicherry, we lost a carton which had all of my mother's novels and also my secret diary. I heard my father scold the movers and packers on the telephone and when I questioned him regarding the same, he quoted their manager's words, "We will try our best to get you back your belongings", which I had heard on the speakerphone. It's been five days and we have not heard a word about it from the manager. Meantime, I decided to redecorate a hard-bounded book that I had lying in my pile of notebooks for a long time now. As far as my memory, I had purchased this from a local exhibition.

Another subsequent reason as to why I am not looking forward to coming back to Mumbai lies in the word- 'back'. This is not the first time I will be staying in Mumbai. In fact, I was born and brought up in this city of dreams. It was around ten months ago that my father got a job posting in Pondicherry. I was at first sad when I heard about the relocation. I had all my friends in Mumbai, I had spent a major part of my life growing up here. It was not a change I was up for. It was, however, a change inevitable. The initial few weeks in Pondicherry were tough. I had to interview in four different schools, got rejected from two, my parents did not like one, hence due to lack of choice, the fourth school, Villow High School, was where I was enrolled.

As a child studying in eighth grade, this sudden transition was a lot to take in, even though I understood its necessity. There was a sudden shift in the classroom culture. The diversity of students in VHS, short form for Villow High School was quite different from the students I grew up with. However, going by the saying, time heals all, as time flew by, I did eventually settle in and mixed with my peers well. It did not seem all that bad. It was a change, but it was a good change. Not only was I socially coping up well with the situation, I was also academically doing better than I did back in Mumbai.

Within a span of two months, this place felt more like home. It was more comforting and I felt more relaxed and myself here. It was a feeling that I still do not understand but it was nice. The friends I made in Pondicherry liked me a lot, I think. In my Mumbai school, they were all my friends, but they kept secrets from me. I did feel left out at times, but I was habitual to it. If not anything, it felt very normal and okay. But whenever I gave them one of my stationery, like once I gave them my favourite pen, it had a red body with a pink cap with a blinking star on the top, they did not keep any secrets from me that day. In fact, they told me a few of their secrets. That feeling was very nice. But in Pondicherry, everybody told me their secret even if I did not give them any of my belongings. Nobody told me to sit alone for a lecture because they wanted to discuss something with the others. Nobody made fun of my appearance as well, it was very awkward at first. In Mumbai, I was always called by names such as 'Hockey stick', 'Bugs Bunny', 'Flat tree', 'Lizard' or 'Miss Boney bones', the most common one. When I heard these names for the first time, I was very hurt but then I heard my friends address others with such names too and it felt better. It was their way of telling us that they consider us as their friends, I inferred. It was strange at times that keeping aside a close group of five girls, they addressed all the others with such words rather than their actual name. In Pondicherry, I was, however, addressed by my own name. Everyone called me Siara or lovingly also Sia at times. It was nice hearing my own name, I really like my name. Another predominant change was that in Mumbai my friends always ate half of my tiffin while I was in the washroom, washing my hands. The washroom trip during lunch break would roughly take around ten minutes, we had to stand in queue and maintain the decorum, these were strict instructions given to us each day by our teachers. My friends from Mumbai always said that they really liked the food my mother packs for me. Many times, they loved it so much that they would finish it without me but in return they would also let me sit next to them the entire day and give me a piece of their chocolate as well. In Pondicherry, everyone waits for each other during lunch break and all my friends shared their tiffin with me as well. It is a lot of fun to take a bite from everyone's tiffin and taste different food each day. Additionally, I also get to sit with them, which was always great.

One rainy evening, I came back home after playing with my building friends. Yes, I made two friends in my building too. On returning home that particular evening, the atmosphere in the house wasn't the usual. My parents were having a serious discussion with my brother about something. Seeing me enter the house, my father said, "Very good you are back home as well, your mother and I have been meaning to tell you both some news. I have taken up a new job offer, and they are posting me in Mumbai. We are shifting back to Mumbai in a month!", this was followed by lightning and thundering outside, scaring me to bits. My brother seemed pretty happy on hearing this news and so were my parents thrilled to deliver it to us but amidst all this rejoicing, I was sad. This sudden blow of fear hit me, I felt it. Even now that we are back in my hometown, that fear has not left. I tried talking my parents out of this, but there is only little a fourteen-year-old can do.

June 14, 2008

It has been over a week since we moved back to Mumbai. My brother got himself enrolled back in the same school we studied in previously. I, on the other hand, convinced my parents to not get me admitted in that school. I wanted to join some other school, any other school. My brother was very happy to be back in town, he contacted all his friends and hadn't been this ecstatic in a long time. I had not told anybody about my return. I fail to understand why I am taking such steps, but I know for sure that I do not want to enter that school. This was a kind of fear quite different from the one I had before entering VHS.

Okay, I have to go now, we are visiting a bunch of schools all across the town to see if they can give me admission. Fingers crossed!

June 17, 2008

We have visited seven different schools until now. All schools have already started, and they all refuse to give me admission. They told my parents that they were sorry and that they do not take any new admissions at this point in time. My father requested them to make an exception but all in vain. It has left us with only one option, I join my previous school back. My parents are clueless about my resentment, just as I am. A few hours ago my mother came into my room, while I sat on the edge of the bed, crying, dreading going back to the same building I had left earlier. She gave me the assurance that everything is going to be alright and said that I am looking too much into the matter. Let us hope for the best.

June 19, 2008

Today was my first day at school, the same school I had left months ago. I did not sleep last night. I pretended to be sick this morning as well but my mother caught my lie within seconds. My father dropped me and my brother at the school gate. I refused to get out of the car seat complaining about chronic back pain but as usual, this tactic failed as well. Very reluctantly I entered the school. We have an assembly every morning where all students assemble on the school ground. There are prayers followed by some news, positive and inspirational thoughts, pledge and finally concluded with the National Anthem. When we reached, the teachers were instructing all students to stand in a queue, class-wise and height-wise. The class monitor was holding the division board uptight and high in the sky for all the students to spot their class with ease. I quickly found my class's division board and went and stood in the line. There were some known and some unknown faces, all turned towards me. While some seemed shocked to see me out of nowhere, some were baffled. Nobody was happy or was smiling, I could tell. I wanted to run away to Pondicherry. I know it in my heart that all the faces there would have greeted me with a smile if not anything else. I stood there in the line, with my eyes transfixed at the ground. Throughout the assembly program, all I did was stand there, making shapes with my right leg on the muddy ground. I could not gather the guts to look up straight.

However, the worst was yet to come. When I reached my classroom, I saw the same group of friends that I had left behave very similarly to how they did previously. They were still calling others by names other than the one their parents had given them. This would have been a very normal sight for the Siara who was in this school eleven months ago. However, for this Siara who was back after being a student of VHS, it was not a good sight. I did not want to engage with them, anymore. I tried dodging eye contact with anybody and just hoped to get to any empty seat as soon as possible. While I searched for an empty seat, I felt a tap on my left shoulder. I looked towards my left, in the meantime, one of my old friends grabbed my lunch bag that I held in the right hand and snatched it from me. All of this happened before I could bat an eyelid. I did not know how to react. From the corner of my eye, I spotted an empty seat on the rightmost column of benches and ran to catch it as soon as I could. I did not turn behind or even confront them, I just ran. I could see faces turn and heard giggles and whispers throughout the lectures. All I did was look down and just fill the pages of my notebook with running notes.

The mid-day lunch break bell rang, and I was there at my desk, still writing something in my notebook. I was hungry. By this time in Pondicherry, everyone would be ready with their open tiffin boxes, ready to dive right into it. I was by now used to having an entire meal all by myself in the afternoons. I used to eat all the food that my mother packed for me, each day. During break time, nobody came to me to offer their tiffin. I did see a girl trying to approach me but before she could talk to me, my old friends called her to them. I do not know why this was happening. Actually, now that I think about it, this is exactly what always happened, it is just that I did not avoid them earlier. The old me would definitely go to them for my tiffin box and laugh the entire episode off. The new me did not want to do any of that. My entire day at school was more or less like this.

I came back home, famished, wanting to eat anything and everything that was cooked by my mother. Yet, when I was served the food, I do not know why I was not able to gulp it down. It was a very strange feeling. My stomach was making noises, even then when I put the food in my mouth, I was facing great difficulty chewing it and swallowing it. I might have eaten just half of what was served to me when my mother noticed this. She asked me why I was not eating my food at my regular pace, I had no reply. "I am not hungry, I ate a lot at school today", was my excuse.

June 20, 2008

Today, our Mathematics teacher, took a surprise test in class on the topic Ratio and Proportion. Luckily for me, I had covered this topic back in Pondicherry, so I aced the test and also mathematics is my favourite subject. This was my first test post my return and my teacher, Sukhwinder sir, was rather impressed with my performance considering how I had missed the initial weeks. He also gave me a chocolate for my performance. It was nice to eat a chocolate during the break today. Even my mother was very happy about my result. However, at first, she scolded me for not informing her earlier and was slightly upset that she had to find out about it while she emptied my bag of any wrappers or waste papers.

I do not know why but I do not feel like talking a lot nowadays. I have always been very talkative. There was a time when I used to come back home and spend at least an hour, if not more, narrating the events that occurred through the course of my day at school to my mother and repeat the same at night when my father would return from work. Even in Primary School, the only complain my teachers ever had from me was that I would distract my fellow classmates by talking to them during the lecture. But now, I just feel like staying in bed all day either drawing something in my notebook or watching the television. Howbeit, my mother does not approve of this behaviour of me.

Even writing this diary on a daily basis is getting a little hard for me. I don't know.

Okay, I have nothing else to say today, it is time to sleep.

June 26, 2008

I almost forgot about this diary until now, when I have been instructed to stay in my room for the next two hours as a punishment by my parents. While the daily bag cleaning today, my mother checked my school calendar and found three negative remarks from my schoolteachers. Two of them were from my class teacher, both mentioning that I had failed to submit my homework on time, and one was from Sukhwinder sir, who wrote about my inattentiveness in class. "This is shocking, why have you hidden these remarks from me? You haven't gotten a single remark earlier. This is very disappointing", sighed my mother. She kept asking me to justify this casual attitude that I was imbibing. I had no replies to any of her worries.

It is exceedingly difficult for me to focus on anything nowadays. Things are not as they were earlier. Nobody talks to me in school. Just like early times, all my old friends take my tiffin, each day, but they do not offer me a piece of their chocolate or offer me a seat next to theirs. Everyone is a part of some group and are almost all the time just busy among themselves. I am hardly even noticed now. The only thing that is constant is my name at school which still happens to be 'Miss Boney bones'.

Every morning I struggle to get out of bed. I spend the entire night thinking of ways, making excuses to miss school the following day but as soon as the alarm rings and I see my brother at my bedroom's doorstep waiting to wake me up, I fall short of words, I feel suffocated, choked on words. All I am able to do is push myself out of bed. I am unable to express myself to anybody. I do realize that things are a little different now or is it just me who is acting differently? If I go to see, everything around me does seem the same, it seems normal. Then, in that case, do I need to start being normal? I am failing deeply to understand anything at this point in time.

Just heard my mother call out my name, looks like punishment period is over now.

Oh, and also tomorrow in the assembly I have to read out a positive quote. The student for this responsibility is usually selected at random by using the lucky draw system, and it so happened that it was my roll number that was written in the chit drawn out today. While my teacher seemed very happy to hand this opportunity to me, I am numb on the inside. I feel like a blank slate. This is not the first time I will be addressing a crowd, ever since I was in primary school, I have always participated in elocution and extempore competitions. So, I know that I am not nervous, it is just that I feel nothing about it right now.

Okay, heard my name for the second time in a row now, it is getting late, I have to go.

June 28, 2008

I am not really allowed to write anything right now as the doctor advised me complete bed rest for the next three days at least but I am bored and also quite contented right now about the fact that I do not have to attend school till I completely recover so I thought I might as well write this piece of good news down.

Today morning, while I was reading out the inspirational quote something bizarre occurred. Halfway through reading the quote, I might have read out four words approximately, I sensed the ground around me tilt a little and before I knew anything, I blanked out and hit the ground. Figuring out from the best of my knowledge, I had fainted. My teachers took me to the medical room, and I was examined by the doctor there. Soon, my mother was called in and I woke up to a conversation between the two. While the doctor at first suspected that I had fallen ill because I had probably not eaten anything in the morning, my mother assured him that she had shoved down food through my throat in the morning. Yes, noticing my poor eating habits lately, mother had taken upon herself to feed me food, both in the morning and at night. A little secret, between you and me, most of the times I used to vomit the food out. I did not do it intentionally but as I have mentioned earlier, most of the times I could not gulp down the food. The doctor then checked my body temperature and weight and informed my mother that I was underweight and wrote down a dietary plan for me and a prescribed a list of medicines that I have to consume for the following three days and suggested complete bed rest.

On our way back home, my mother looked at me with worried eyes and said, "Oh Siara, look at you! You have become so weak. You will have to take care of yourself, honey." And kissed me on the cheek and gave me a warm hug. I always liked warm hugs from my parents and brother. They are very comforting and relaxing. I get it all the time, in the morning before leaving for school and at night before going to bed. However, this one felt different, I mean, it was the same, but I felt different from within. I just hugged her back tightly and cried my heart out. She asked me was I physically in any pain, I denied and just continued crying, did not utter a word, just let the tears roll down my cheeks.

When we were home, I felt better. I think the medicines were doing their magic. Even now as I write in the diary, I feel more relaxed than usual.

July 1, 2008

I have to attend school from tomorrow! Back to the dreadful routine. I do not want to go to school, the last four days have been the best. I played computer games, drew so many drawings, painted a lot of them and also saw a movie. It was so much fun, staying at home and enjoying. A rejuvenation that was much needed. I had two full bowls of amazing mutton porridge in the afternoon today. It felt so nice. I hope I fall ill tomorrow or something, please God!

July 13, 2008

Today is officially the worst day ever! I had my mock tests in school today. I did not perform well, and my class teacher sent the analysed reports of the same to my parents. To be honest, I do not enjoy studying anymore. I do not feel like doing anything in class than just sit at one place and doodle in my notebook. What is the big deal in that? My parents scolded me for a good one hour today. They told me that they were disappointed in me and that I had changed, I was not the same Siara that I was before. Well, guess what? I know that I have changed, that is a no brainer, I feel. They kept asking me why I had turned into this person, why I had started keeping things to myself, why am I being this aloof from everything and everybody, why I was not taking care of myself, why things that once excited me have no effect on me right now? I could not answer any of those questions. These were questions that had time and again hit me as well and I have always been unable to answer them myself.

The other day while returning from school, my brother saw me crying. "Siara, what happened? What is wrong? Did somebody say something to you? Did somebody do something? Tell me?", he asked. I had no answer. "No, brother. Honestly, I do not know if there is something wrong, I do not know if somebody said something to me, I do not know if somebody did something to me, I do not know." I felt like saying. "No, there is nothing", I replied. There is something atypical, that I know for sure, but the answer to what it is, is something that does not lie with me.

Anyway, being agitated for not getting a reply, my mother banned me from watching television and decided to monitor my studies, like how she did in grade five or six, while my father decided to take away all my colouring books. How can they take away my colouring books? Those are mine! This is so frustrating.

July 14, 2008

This is day 1, without my colouring book but thank God I have my diary with me. I am actually writing in my diary for the first time in class. I was always afraid of carrying the diary with me to school because I did not want anybody to take it away from me. I do not want to draw any attention to it. Therefore, I covered it with brown cover this morning, so that it seems like any other notebook. Right now, the Mathematics lecture is going on and Sir has given us a few problems to solve but I have no idea about them, as usual. In most classes, I do not understand anything except in Art and Craft class but after the incident last week, I have decided to exclude myself from that class.

My teacher really seemed to like my work and she decided to showcase my drawings as an example and guidelines for the rest of the class, this drew a lot of unwanted attention towards me and my work. I did not like it. I had many students come up to me and praise me which I am sure were all sugar-coated sarcastic comments. Who in this school has ever spoken to me like that anyway? As expected, this did not last long as well. My old friends, who by now have completely abandoned me because wait, I am still trying to figure that out, were quick enough to shoo everyone who had gathered around me to see more of my artwork. Out of the entire incident, the part where everybody goes back to doing what they were initially doing was the most normal thing that happened that day. So, I have joined the Bookclub that has book reading sessions every Wednesday at 1pm same as Arts and Craft class timings for division A. There is nothing that has to be done during the book reading session than just sit at one place and hear the overly enthusiastic students read out a part of their favourite book. This basically means more doodling or now that my colouring book is gone more writing time for me. Life's Good!

Oh, the bell just rang! It is finally time to head back home.

I came back home two hours ago, and I have been asked to sit down to study almost immediately after lunch was served. Right now, I have been asked to complete my Geography and History home assignments and I am clueless about the same, so I started rewriting my diary.

August 3, 2008

Finally got my diary back! The exams are over too.

I am sorry for the abrupt ending in my last entry, I was caught writing in my diary rather than doing my homework, so I had that taken away from me as well. At first, it was very difficult to do anything during school and at home but soon enough thanks to my books reading session at school, I started reading a lot of books. I am currently done with three Nancy Drew books. In the beginning, I did have a moment of realization about how fragile my attention span was but due to lack of any other forms of distractions that weren't a huge hindrance.

August 7, 2008

My results were declared today. I barely passed in most subjects and failed in one, Mathematics. I could sense my parents being downhearted when they saw the result. It was very heartbreaking, yet I do not know how to resolve it. When we came back home, I expected to be scolded, but to my misery, what I got was the silent treatment.

I came back to my room, not knowing what to do. I did start reading books a few weeks ago but I lost interest in that as well, just like my other short-lived hobbies. Writing this diary is possibly the only thing that I have continued for this long, everything else has been left in the past. Every day is a new struggle. I do not know what I should hustle for if the hustle is even worth it. I am just a skinny girl who nobody really cares about. No, it is not that life has just been very cruel to me. A few days ago, we hosted my brother's birthday party at my place. Most of our guests were our relatives along with a few of his friends. Many people complimented the way I looked that day. My mother had spent the entire afternoon to doll me up. Normally, people feel good about themselves when they dress up or when complimented, I just felt numb on the inside. There was a dance floor being set up in the living room, we hired a jukebox playing one of the best dance playlists ever, few of which were songs that I had performed to either during my school dance performances or some family get together. I remember enjoying them to the fullest back in the day but when they were played at this party, I did not feel that adrenaline rush or have any motivation to dance. I just found myself in a corner observing everything. Amidst the music around, that felt more like chaos, my brain seemed to register nothing, it just saw smiling faces around me without knowing how to comprehend anything.

I feel exhausted right now. Completely drained, both mentally and physically. I do not know how to push myself anymore. How to wake up in the morning not wanting to ever leave the bed? Do my parents deserve this? I see them trying so hard to get back the Siara they brought up. Well, I am sorry, I have lost her somewhere never to be seen again. I do not want to be the reason for their sorrow. I cannot cry any more, my eyes have dried up. I do not deserve any happiness now, do I?

May 08, 2019

Today was the first seminar that I conducted as a Psychology major. I read out this very diary that I am writing right now in, in front of a crowd of two hundred students, aspiring to become lawyers, doctors, engineers, artists or even social activists in the future. I went on the stage with no expectations, my only aim was to spread awareness about mental illness and to preach the concept that nobody is alone. I realized through life experiences that it is okay to feel hollow on the inside and it is one hundred percent possible to emerge victorious out of it. There is always light at the end of the tunnel is what I have strongly started believing in.

Before anything, I want to thank the fourteen-year-old Siara for writing in this diary for as long as she could. For not giving up on herself, for always having the strength to get up each morning and fight the unresolved internal and external conflicts. I cannot appreciate her enough for her bravery to sail through the storm. She has done the Powerpuff Girls proud. I thank her for not letting the thoughts of end take over her, irreversibly. I thank her for opening up in front of her loved ones when the situation tried to close her up forever. Without this will power, I would not be able to experience what beauty this place can hold alongside the doldrums. I can now acknowledge my own capabilities. I fathom the change I can bring. I understand the gravity and importance of the sunshine that I can bring in the life of million Siaras, fighting each day, each hour and each second in their life. I thank her for helping me live this new life. She is the reason why I realized that no matter how cloudy it gets, there can and will be a bright sunny day, sooner or later.

I can never be any less grateful to everybody who has been a part of this journey. Be it the people who impacted my past life negatively or the amazing souls who helped me get to this place. It is the combination of the two that has helped Siara reach here. They have not only helped my past self-change her own life but also the life of the countless other Siaras, belonging to many different age groups or genders. The reason for their suffering may differ, largely and widely, but their fight against the conflict remains the same, each day, each minute.

Also, a huge thank you from the audience today and many more to come, who connect with your story, who you help to see that this is not the end for them. A thank you from the teared-up people, who you gave the strength to pick themselves up, who now know they are not alone, who now know they do deserve happiness, who now know it is okay to not know at times. I cannot ever thank you enough.

With Love,
Siara.

ITS ALL ABOUT STORIES, SO WRITE/ DRAW/

SCRIBBLE A STORY THAT YOU HEARD RECENTLY.

IT CAN EVEN BE AN INCIDENT THAT YOUR FRIEND

TOLD YOU ABOUT.

ACKNOWLEDGEMENTS

Imagine what all we could conquer if we stopped criticizing and started supporting each other. I am one of those lucky people who had a strong and great backbone during this project. It was so amazing to have such an incredible senior like Anush Goel who was so open to all of my ideas whether they were good or bad, he listened to all of them. He had faith in me during this whole time and always motivated me to give my 100% to this project. Just like any human, I had my ups and downs during this project and without this belief, I wouldn't have been able to complete this book. Secondly, I would like to acknowledge all the writers who kept their calm during this lengthy process and had full faith in me and Inkfeathers and for giving out such incredible stories for the book. It wouldn't be possible without them. Last but not the least, I had two underdogs helping me in this project with no intentions of being recognized or plans for earning anything, just with the intention of helping a friend and with a heart full of love. Srushti Deekonda and Jyotsna Ramachandran, without you girls I swear I would have just broken down. You girls were the best thing that happened to me during this project. Thank you so much for helping me out through this whole process, it means the world to me.

ABOUT THE AUTHORS

1. Sindhuja Sarasram

She considers herself a regular girl who loves antiquity, travel, soulful words, bright ideas, great big romances, and fur babies, basically, things that leave behind imprints (definitely paw prints!) on the soul. With the desire to make a mark herself, she chose Architecture. Gate-crashing her wedding with a 9-5 job now, are writing & art. So, she's a bad person who's greedy for 'em three.

2. Aparnaa Thanigai

To describe herself, she would like to quote Katy Perry, "Like a plastic bag, drifting through the wind, wanting to start again". When she is not brooding or drowning in existential crisis, she dabbles at writing. She is an aspiring globetrotter (fingers crossed she makes it before the apocalypse, although the odds don't seem to be in her favour), she loves baking (desserts are her kryptonite) and she also loves talking, as evidenced by her rambling bio. It is her fervent hope to be adopted by a dog one day.

3. Sanyogita Bharadwaj

She is currently pursuing her Bachelor of Arts in Psychology, Journalism and Literature. She believes music is therapy to the soul and books are the fuel to an active imagination. She's an aspiring Clinical Psychologist. She believes - "Be it a battle with yourself or the world, no matter how big or small, love and a little more love is just enough to conquer.

4. Kanika Choudhary

She is the creator of 'Profoundwords_', a content blog on Instagram, featuring innovative quotes and fragments of poetry relating to all generations, open to everyone. Although she's an aspiring UX / UI designer, writing has always been an integral part of her life. Her work has already been published in an anthology called 'Adolescenes- A Risky Drive' published by Inkfeathers.

5. Sree Yelamanchi

A doctor by profession and writer by passion. She chose writing to get through the dark days of her life, eventually fell in love with it and that is when she started to believe it's not you that chooses writing, but it's writing that chooses you. Books, coffee, and chocolate are her happy place and she plans to live the rest of her life taking it as and how it comes, just one day at a time.

6. Amol Gawade

He is from Dahisar, Mumbai. Civil Engineer by profession. Humanity is a religion for him. Always looks for inspiration from moments of life, sharing his positive thoughts through his Amulya Vichaar. Loves to travel, trek & write positive thoughts. Always believes in karma, and is looking forward to positive things, better days. For him, "You get in life what you have the courage to experience."

7. Arati Harikumar

Arati is an HR professional who tries (hard too!) to pursue many hobbies. A reader by day and writer by night, a dancer over the weekends and a traveller when a destination beckons; she loves wearing many hats. She is currently working with Deloitte India and can be reached at LinkedIn.

8.   Shagun Salecha

She is currently pursuing her Masters in Geoinformatics and has a Bachelor's in Geography. Writing is something that helps her to introspect herself. She believes that it is one beautiful piece of art that makes her understand the different sides of each coin. It reflects a person's inner self that's portrayed on a piece of paper. A famous quote by Profoundwords, "Let's chase the colours of the rainbow together" has helped her to find diversity in her life and pass through various difficulties as well. She is an energetic girl who loves to remain outdoors and socialize. She derives a sense of motivation by helping others.

9.   Pritha Samanta

Some believe in God, some in the universe. Pritha believes in stories and dreams. An architect by profession, Pritha likes to conjure situations and settings as a full-time job. When not working, she finds ways to satisfy her wanderlust or stand behind the kitchen counter to conjure some lip-smacking dishes.

10. Simran Saxena

She is a 22-year-old dreamer with a bundle of aspirations. One such aspiration is to be able to propagate a positive attitude towards a rather taboo topic of mental illness. Professionally, she is a budding Engineer but passionately she wants to always be that lending ear that people can talk to. Her other hobbies include swimming, travelling, dancing, and public speaking.

11. Vanshika Agarwal

A wanderer at heart, and wants to write her heart out, more for the world and less as a means of an escape. A Firm believer of Hope, and that it has ways to show up in the most unexpected times in Life. She believes best stories are the age-old stories, writers only portray their perspectives.

12. Anurag Kumar

Anurag is 33-years-old who is working as an Assistant Professor Contractual in Medininagar, Daltonganj, Jharkhand.

Our Story

We're all on a journey, and our "Writers" have made it Beautiful.

A dreamcatcher is an object made with feathers and strings, essentially used as lucky charms in many parts of the world. The same way, Inkfeathers brings together writers, editors, and artists together to form a dreamcatcher that works in favour for the young writers and readers and if you're positive about it, it may bring you luck as well.

We at Inkfeathers are connected with thousands of writers globally, who believe in the magic of telling stories. This stream of connectivity with the writers, the fact that everyone has a unique detail or edge to their story makes Inkfeathers proud to partner with these young literary as well as collaborative minds.

Back in 2013, our founders came together to form an offline group for their love of literature, and this formed collaborative energy with many young literature-wounded minds which eventually led these offline meetings to stand-ups, storytelling events, poetry slams, meet-ups to share experiences and many others. In 2016, Inkfeathers finally launched as the brand project under one Private Limited Company. This expanded opportunity gave a number of possibilities and a new way to expand our support for writers.

This dream of wanting to bring together writers as well as readers has come true beyond measure as writers connect to us from countries like United States, United Kingdom, Canada each day to bring their story to life.

As of this year, we are extremely delighted to provide you with our website (www.inkfeathers.com) where all your queries can be resolved about our self-publishing process and latest anthologies. You can get hold of the latest updates on anthologies, events, offers, new book releases and so much more here. You can go ahead and order a book from our bookstore to get a taste of our mindful curation of stories and poems.

Inkfeathers Publishing family encourages you to really put your feelings out there in words for the world to see, in order to have a common ground to grow mutually. We are a creative platform for all those seeking literary help in terms of having their words published.

Believe us, publishing a book is not easy, but we come to a writer's rescue at each phase of having their book in print in terms of Editing, Designing, Branding, Marketing and all the other work that goes behind until you have a printed copy in your hands for Distribution. Together, it couldn't have been any easier. We will be there for you, to help you turn your manuscript into a freshly bound book that sells off the glass bookshelves.

With Love,
Inkfeathers Publishing